EMIRATES
CABIN CREW
INTERVIEW
MADE EASY

EMIRATES
CABIN CREW
INTERVIEW
MADE EASY

CAITLYN ROGERS

SPINEBOUND BOOKS

EMIRATES Cabin Crew Interview Made Easy

Second Edition by Caitlyn Rogers,
Copyright © 2014 Caitlyn Rogers

Published by:
SpineBound Books
United Kingdom

ISBN: 978-1-908300-13-3

Printed in the United Kingdom
10 9 8 7 6 5 4 3 2 1

Library of Congress Cataloging-in-Publication Data
A CIP catalogue record for this book can be obtained from the
British Library

SPINEBOUND BOOKS

www.SpineBound.co.uk

"Who said it could not be done? And what great victories has he to his credit which qualify him to judge others accurately?

- Napoleon Hill"

PART 1

THE ASSESSMENT PROCESS

PART 2

MAKE YOURSELF UNFORGETTABLE

PART 3

BOOST YOUR CANDIDACY

PART 4

LIFTING THE LID ON THE GROUP INTERVIEW

PART 5

TAKE ON THE FINAL INTERVIEW

PART 6
QUESTIONS AND ANSWERS

Disclaimer
FROM THE PUBLISHER

This book is designed to provide information and guidance on attending the cabin crew assessment with Emirates® Airlines. It is sold with the understanding that the publisher and author are not engaged in rendering legal or other professional services. Such topics, as discussed herein are for example or illustrative purposes only. If expert assistance is required the services of a competent professional should be sought where you can explore the unique aspects of your situation and can receive specific advice tailored to your circumstances.

It is not the purpose of this guide to reprint all the information that is otherwise available to candidates but instead to complement, amplify and supplement other texts. You are urged to read all the available material, learn as much as possible about the role and interview techniques and tailor the information to your individual needs.

Every effort has been made to make this guide as complete and accurate as possible, however, this guide contains information that is current only up to the printing date. Interview processes are frequently updated and are often subject to differing interpretations, therefore, there are no absolutes and this text should be used only as a general guide and not as the ultimate source of information.

Get updates
ONLINE

Updates, special offers and newsletters will be made available at:

www.CabinCrew.guide

So be sure to stop by.

www.CabinCrew.Guide

Where dreams are made

My Dedication

TO YOU

This book is dedicated to all my readers who refuse to give up on their dream.

Thank you and good luck

THE ASSESSMENT
PROCESS
PART I

Contents
Of this Session

1. The truth about the hiring process

2. What Emirates are looking for

3. What to expect

The truth

ABOUT THE HIRING PROCESS

We'd all like to think that recruitment personnel are giving their undivided attention to each resume they receive, and we'd also like to think that every candidate would receive a fair and equal opportunity to interview for the position. The unfortunate truth is, Emirates is "Swamped with cabin crew applications" (Gulf News, 2010). It is quoted that the airline receives over 15,000 applications each and every month, with most recruitment drives attracting upwards of 1,000 applicants. The Chief Commercial Officer of Emirates, Thierry Antinori, noted that Emirates received over 129,000 applications during 2013 alone. (Trade Arabia, 2014).

In fact, it is recorded that of the 400 candidates who turned up to a 2010 open day in Spain, just 30 made it though to the final interview, and it is a good guess that not all 30 of those were ultimately hired.

While this is undeniably a substantial number of applicants, Emirates are a large and expanding airline with plenty of vacancies to fill. So why does the success rate remain so very low?

In order to understand these failure rates, it helps to understand things from the airline and recruitment officer's perspective. So let's take a look at things from the another point of view.

The airline's
PERSPECTIVE

After seeing hundreds of hopefuls, it is only natural that faces and resumes begin to blur, with each sounding and looking much the same as the next. This not only puts a great deal of pressure on recruitment teams to reduce the load, but also makes it very difficult for any one candidate to stand out.

To address this overload, Emirates have become highly selective and candidates are put through a gruelling screening process, whereby large numbers of unsuspecting candidates are eliminated as early as possible.

When you consider that most people will enter the process without any prior preparation, and some don't even meet the basic requirements of the position, it is easy to understand why the failure rates remain high.

In reading this book and taking the time to prepare, you can avoid being culled by the process and will stand out as someone who not only cares about the position, but also has respect for the recruiter's time.

Work the system
TO YOUR ADVANTAGE

By understanding the process from the inside, **you can avoid being slaughtered by these underhand tactics.** You can tip the balance of power in your favour, so that you become the one who is doing the screening, not the airline. **No longer will you be cursed with generic run-of-the-mill answers and uninspiring resumes that have you looking and sounding like everyone else,** but will stand out as the top candidate that you truly are.

So whether you are a seasoned applicant who is finding yourself frustrated by another unsuccessful attempt or are a new candidate looking forward to your first interview, the **insider secrets and step by step guidance** within this book will give you a huge lead over the competition.

What Emirates
ARE LOOKING FOR

"What are they looking for?" is the one question I am asked, time and time again. So many candidates overanalyse the process, but the answer is actually very simple. Put simply, Emirates are looking for the right candidates for their current circumstances.

If you visit Emirates website, you will find the criteria for the position of cabin crew is openly published and available to view. The guidelines are very simple and often outline key elements, which fall into the following categories Eligibility, suitability and specific criteria. Put together these three elements form a 'Person Specification' which recruiters use to determine if a candidate is suitable or not.

The person
SPECIFICATION

Eligibility

Eligibility checks are based on facts that can be determined either by physical or documentary evidence.

Eligibility checks, as noted on the Emirates website, include:

- At least 21 years of age at the time of joining
- Arm reach of 212 cm while standing on tiptoes
- High school graduate (Grade 12)
- Fluency in English (Written and Spoken)
- No visible tattoos while in Emirates Cabin Crew uniform (cosmetic and bandage coverings not permitted)
- Physically fit to meet the Emirates Cabin Crew requirements

Suitability

Unlike eligibility which is based on facts, suitability involves identifying the right personal qualities.

These are defined by Emirates as:

- A positive attitude and empathy for others
- Strong cultural awareness and the ability to adapt to new environments and people
- Flexibility and the motivation to manage a demanding work schedule
- Qualities – Professional, Empathetic, Progressive, Visionary, Cosmopolitan

Specific requirements

Eligibility and Suitability are basic requirements, which must be met in all cases. Emirates then proceed to customise their specific requirements according to their own needs and standards. If, for example, Emirates identifies that an increase in the number of language speakers is required, then language ability may be given precedence.

In order to avoid disappointment, you are recommended to investigate the current requirements carefully before applying. There is no excuse for not meeting the basic requirements, and you will be eliminated if you don't meet those given.

Physical

PROFILE

Due to the general physical nature of the job, Emirates have stringent health and fitness guidelines in place for its cabin crew. You will be required to undertake comprehensive medical examinations, so it is important to be mindful of these before you apply.

Health and fitness

As glamorous as the job appears, your health will be affected from the lack of routine, climatic and time zone changes, and long working hours so good health and strong immune system is essential for dealing with these conditions. In addition, you will need a good overall level of fitness for dealing with the general physical nature of the job, which includes opening and closing emergency doors and standing for long periods.

Hearing

An audiogram must be provided prior to joining and must cover the 500-3000Hz range. You should not have a hearing loss, in either ear separately, of more than 35db at any of the frequencies 500, 1,000, 2,000Hz or more than 50db at 3,000Hz. However, a hearing loss greater than the above may be declared fit providing:

• The applicant has a hearing performance in each ear separately equivalent to that of a normal person, against a background noise that will stimulate the masking properties of flight deck noise upon speech and beacon signals; and

• The applicant has the ability to hear an average conversation voice in a quiet room using both ears, at a distance of 2 meters (6 feet) from the examiner, with the back turned to the examiner

Eyesight

The following are the requirements for eye sight of Emirates cabin crew

*   Good Binocular Vision
*   Distant Visual Acuity, with correction by contact lenses
    (if necessary), to 6/9 (20/30) or better
*   Near Vision Acuity, with correction by contact lenses (if necessary),
    to read N5 at 30-50cm and N14 at 100cm
*   Currently, spectacles cannot be worn and so only contact lenses
    are acceptable for visual correction. These lenses should be
    suitable for long-term wear in the dry aircraft environment. Soft
    permeable lenses are preferable and those candidates who require
    hard lenses (e.g. keratoconus) are not suitable.

Height

Emirates no longer specify a specific height requirement, as this has been replaced with an arm reach requirement instead. The current standard of reach is set at 212cm on tip-toes and in bare feet.

To determine your reach ability, a simple reach test will be conducted during the course of the assessment, whereby a mark is placed on the wall and you will be asked to reach for the line. Failure to reach the mark will result in your dismissal from the event, there are no exceptions.

I cannot stress the importance of conducting a reach test before you apply, as many candidates arrive to the event only to discover that they do not meet this basic requirement. It is a simple test that can save you much time, effort and expense.

Increase your height

If you conduct a reach test and discover that you cannot reach the line, this does not mean that you can never become cabin crew, it simply means that you need to put some time and effort into increasing your height. Yes, you did read that correctly. With regular stretching excercises and practicing yoga routines, it has been documented that an individual can increase their height by as much as 1-2 inches in just a matter of weeks. Try it and see for yourself.

Weight

While it is a myth that airlines only hire candidates who embody perfect figures ,it is important that you maintain a healthy weight in relation to your height. For this purpose, Emirates refer to the Body Mass Index (BMI) guidelines.

The BMI is a formula used by health professionals to determine an adult's healthy body weight in relation to their height. While weight is an avenue that is certainly open to discrimination, particularly for those who fall within the higher end of the spectrum, it is unlikely to be a problem if your weight falls within the mid to lower parameters of the chart. You can determine your own proportions, by referring to the BMI chart that follows.

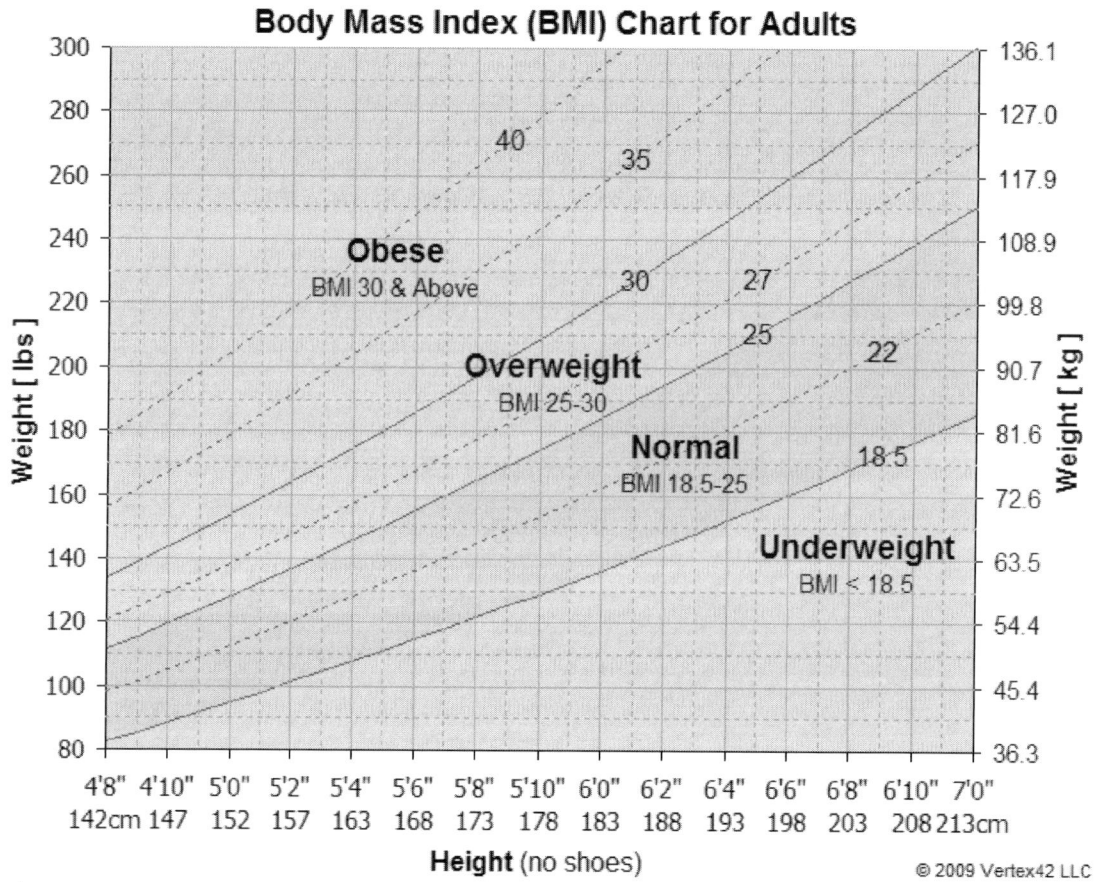

WHAT TO
EXPECT

What to expect

The assessment process varies considerably in length and structure depending on a number of factors. These factors include: The volume of applicants, whether the sessions are held within the airline's premises or a hotel establishment, and whether the sessions are open or invitation only.

Open days typically attract a high volume of candidates and, as such, will often be split over a series of days. Invitation only days, on the other hand, are kept much smaller in number and may span only a few short hours with final interviews conducted on the same day.

In either case, you will be asked to partake is a number of activities. These activities are designed to reveal your personality, competencies and potential for working as cabin crew and are likely to include a series of individual assessments, practical tasks, group discussions and role-play scenarios.

Arrival at the event can seem overwhelming, especially when faced with hundreds of applicants in attendance. You will likely be met with an atmosphere that is friendly and buzzing with adrenaline, but has an eerie sense of tension, as each candidate is anxious to get through the process. This atmosphere generally tapers off as the sessions get underway.

Open day vs
INVITATION ONLY ASSESSMENT

When considering whether to attend an open day or apply for an invitation only session, there are two factors that will determine the best route for you. The first factor lies within the strength of your application, and the second is within your ability to stand out in a crowd.

Invitation only days rely on the pre-screening of applicants to determine suitability. If your resume appears weak, maybe there are large gaps in employment, or an apparent lack of customer service experience, you may be screened out before having an opportunity to explain such weaknesses. While it is possible to strengthen any resume, you may may prefer to bypass the pre-screening and attend an open day instead.

For candidates who struggle within very large groups, maybe due to a lack of assertiveness or a soft voice, the smaller turnout of an invitation only day may be a better match. Within these smaller sessions, it is easier to get involved, and even easier to be seen and heard.

In either case, the rest of this book will provide you with strategies you can use that will strengthen your application and your ability to stand out in a crowd.

A typical
SCHEDULE

There is no set formula as to how many or which combination of activities are included during the Emirates assessment days, however, the process is typically divided into three key segments, these are: Group activities, individual assessments and a panel interview.

Group activities
During the group segment, you will be asked to take part in several activities. These activities are designed to reveal your personality, competencies and potential for working as cabin crew and are likely to include a series of practical tasks, group discussions and role plays.

Individual assessments
Individual assessments may be paper based, such as personality questionnaires and general knowledge tests, or they may be practical, such as self presentations, language proficiency and reach tests. Either way, these assessments form an integral part of the eligibility criteria.

Panel interview
A typical panel interview will take place before two or three recruitment officers. While each member of the panel will have an opportunity to pose questions to the candidate, it is common practice to have a primary examiner to ask questions and a secondary examiner to observe and take notes.

A typical open day will be a two day event and might run as follows:

Day One	
9:00	Arrive, welcome and introductory briefing
9:15	Airline presentation and icebreaker session
10:00	Resume handover
10:55	First eliminations
11:00	Preliminary group session
12:25	Second eliminations
12:30	Lunch break
1:00	Second group session
2:55	Third eliminations
3:00	Individual assessments and mini interview
4:25	Final eliminations
4:30	Debrief
5:00	Depart

Day Two	
9:00 5:00	Day two will typically be filled from 9:00 - 5:00 with blocks of panel interviews. These may be as short as 20 minutes in length, or as long as 2 hours.

A process
OF ELIMINATION

The primary objective during the early stages of the screening process is to filter and eliminate unsuitable candidates as quickly as possible. As such, you will experience periodic elimination sessions throughout much of the day.

The initial eliminations will typically occur shortly after the resume dropoff, then after each group session and individual assessment, but this is by no means absolute as schedules are changed regularly and without notice. In any case, it is this first elimination that is the largest and it is likely that 50% or more will leave the process at this stage.

Naturally the elimination sessions are stressful, but if you make it through the first group round, you can be sure that you have made a positive impression. Now as you go forward to the next round, take comfort in knowing that it will be much easier to stand out with fewer numbers in the group, so build on the impression that you have already created and give it all you've got. Use the adrenaline from your early success to carry you through.

Just a number

Due to the large turnouts, Emirates have negated to assigning candidates with numbers in place of using their names. This system of designation was introduced to streamline the process and to ensure that candidates are regularly shuffled. The idea behind the system is understandable and efficient, however, there is a disadvantage in that it leaves each candidate severely depersonalised. As such, you are no longer Kate, Alexander, Maria or (insert your name here), but instead you are number 284, 879 or 1029.

Such a system makes it all the more essential that you make an effort to stand out and be recognised.

Avoid the traps

DURING THE ICEBREAKER SESSION

The recruitment personnel will often start the day with a video, a short introductory briefing and a breakdown of the intended days events.

During this time, candidates are encouraged to pose questions to the personnel about Emirates and the position.

This session is an ideal opportunity to get noticed early, but it can also be a breaking point for those who are unprepared.

Many of the more confident candidates make the mistake of getting carried away with their line of questioning in an attempt to stand out. Unfortunately, asking too many questions at this stage will only demonstrate a general lack of respect for others, who also have questions, and is also more likely to be misconstrued as arrogant, rather than confident. One question really is sufficient.

In asking questions, there is also the added risk looking ill prepared if a question appears unnecessary or has already been answered within the airline literature. This will highlight your lack of research and does not create a favourable first impression.

If you do not have a valid and effective question, it is better to just listen and observe. There will be many more opportunities to get noticed.

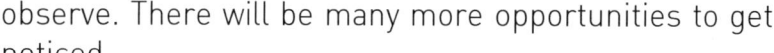

You have 2 minutes

TO IMPRESS

The first interaction you will have with a recruiter is during the resume handover session. While this session may last for an hour or more, each candidate will only be afforded 2 minutes each to hand over their resume and make a positive and memorable impression. First eliminations may take place on this basis alone, so it is important that you make your time in the limelight as memorable as you possibly can.

Most importantly, remember to observe the officer's name and use it when you introduce yourself. Here is an example:

"Hello Judith, my name is Caitlyn and I appreciate the time you have taken to meet with me today."

While this may sound obvious, or even corney, you'd be surprised to discover how few will introduce themselves in such a pleasing manner. Those who take this initiative will stand out favourably.

Complacency

AND THE WAITING GAME

With large turnouts, the group will often be split into smaller, more manageable sizes, and assessed in rotation. This means that you will likely find yourself waiting around for long periods between sessions. Although you will not be in a formal assessment during these waiting periods, the recruitment officers are still assessing you and it is important to remain professional and alert.

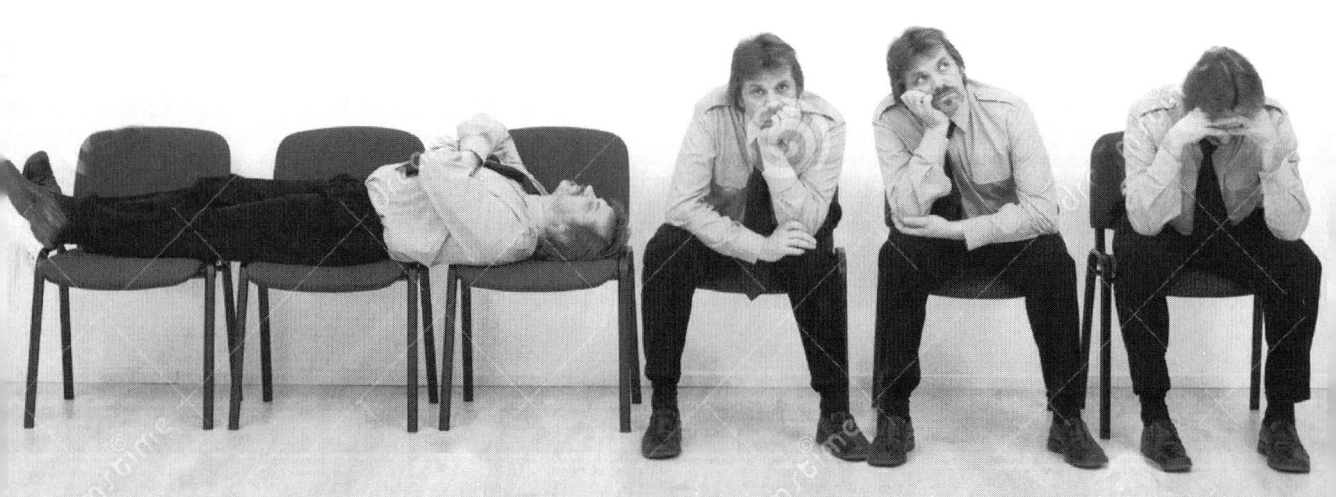

Too many candidates allow themselves to relax during these periods, and it is when they relax too much that they become complacent. Just take a look around next time you are at an event and you will see candidates slouching in their seat and generally looking very bored. Don't allow this to happen to you. Move around and network with the other candidates. This will show that you are taking the event seriously and are a friendly sort. As a side benefit, this will make time pass quicker and make the day much more enjoyable. And don't worry about what other candidates will think, as oftentimes they will appreciate your efforts to lighten the atmosphere.

Session breaks are a welcome relief from the mental and emotional stress that the day can induce, but these are especially risky times for becoming complacent, as many candidates do not realise that they are still being watched and assessed.

Stand out

AS AN INDIVIDUAL

At some stage during the process, you may be asked to provide a self-introduction or introduce a fellow candidate to the group.

As well as learning more about you and your background, these self-introductions are an opportunity for the recruiters to assess how well you cope when addressing a group of people and how articulately you are able to communicate your message while under pressure. In their assessment, they will be looking for good delivery and a certain amount of charisma.

To deliver a presentation that makes an impact, the following page contains some guidelines for you to consider.

Make it relevant

Use this opportunity to highlight your suitability for the job of cabin crew by sharing interesting facts about your present or most recent job, and your motives for making a career change.

Be spontaneous

A self-presentation which is spontaneous, rather than rehearsed, will add life and sincerity to your speech. Sure you can prepare a rough draft and familiarise yourself with it, but don't try to learn it by heart, as there is a risk of appearing forced, dull and robotic.

Inject personality

Show your passion and enthusiasm by injecting some emotion and personality into your presentation.

Be concise

Unless advised otherwise, keep it relatively short and focused. Thirty to Sixty seconds should be sufficient.

Rotate your focus

To give the impression of confidence and engage your audience, rotate your gaze and make eye contact with various members for three to five seconds each, then be sure to redirect your focus back to the recruiters to finish your presentation.

Beware of how you sound

Varying your tone, pitch, volume and pace will eliminate the risk of appearing monotone and make it enjoyable for others to listen to. If you are nervous, you may be more inclined to rush. It will help if you make a deliberate attempt to slow your pace slightly.

Consider this example

" Hi everyone. My name is Caitlyn and it's really nice to meet you all. I'm 27 years old and live in the bustling city of Bristol. I currently work as a freelance hair consultant, which is a job I really enjoy, but I have always wanted to be cabin crew, which is why I am here today. Outside of work, I enjoy horse riding and am captain of the local netball team"

MAKE YOURSELF

UNFORGETTABLE

PART 2

Contents
Of this Session

"A strong, positive self image is the best possible preparation for success"

- Joyce Brothers

POLISH YOUR
APPEARANCE

That all-important
FIRST IMPRESSION

During the first few minutes of meeting you, the recruitment team will make judgements about your character and suitability based on your overall presentation and appearance. This means that your standard of dress, level of grooming and how you portray yourself through your body language and carriage are all being scrutinised. Therefore, if you are to succeed in creating that all-important positive first impression, it is essential that you make an extra effort to establish a presence.

There is no doubt that appearing professional is the key to creating the best impression at a cabin crew interview. The trouble is, being professional is only part of it. Put a robot into a suit and it too would look professional, but would the robot get the job? It is unlikely.

The fact is, airlines are not looking to hire a suit, but rather they are looking to hire an individual with a personality and character. So why do so many candidates arrive at the interview dressed in the same boring attire? Because it is safe and many are afraid to change the status quo.

Think about it for a moment. How many times have you attended an interview only to be faced with countless other black suits and white shirts? Too many to count I'll bet. Suddenly, that feeling of confidence you had when you set out soon vanishes, leaving you feeling like just another face in the sea of people. If you think it's bad from your point of view, just take a look from the recruiter's perspective.

Establishing a presence is much simpler than many realise, but few ever successfully achieve. Why do so few succeed in this vital area? Because of misunderstandings and misinterpretations.

Your appearance

DOES MATTER

When applying for a cabin crew position with Emirates, your appearance is vital. This doesn't mean to imply that Emirates will only hire crew who embody perfect figures and harbour model looks, but there is no denying that Emirates expect applicants and crew to be well groomed and portray a polished image. The trouble with such advice, is that it is too vague and doesn't give a complete picture. This leads to many candidates arriving at the interview, only to be turned away because of something seemingly insignificant.

So, before we continue on, I feel it is important to address and clarify the concerns regarding appearance.

Temporary blemishes and imperfections

For those of you with minor or temporary imperfections, such as the occasional pimple or patch of dry skin, I understand that a spot in the middle of your forehead is not ideal, but it isn't a disaster either. Recruiters are human too and will recognise that this is a temporary imperfection and will not base a hiring decision upon it. Likewise if you have a perceived flaw, such as an unusual face shape, off white teeth or a slightly crooked nose, these are characteristics that make you unique and are highly unlikely to make any sort of impact to the strength of your candidacy. So please stop worrying about extremes and focus your attention on what really matters.

Permanent blemishes and imperfections

On the other hand, if you do have a real concern, such as rosacea, acne, scarring, birthmarks or severely stained teeth, it is unfortunate that such appearance concerns can be cause for elimination, so it really is worthwhile looking into treatments that may be available to you. With the advances in technology, it would appear that nothing is beyond fixing these days, so there is usually a treatment that will work for you.

For scaring, there are non-evasive laser procedures that can drastically minimise their appearance and for acne, there is medication and lotions. For rosacea, dark circles or birthmarks, you will find medical strength concealers and for stained teeth, cosmetic dentistry or tooth whitening procedures. Whatever path you ultimately decide to pursue, it is important to proceed with safety and due consideration.

Tattoos

Tattoos that are visible when in uniform are forbidden, and there are no exceptions to this rule. Tattoos that are hidden and discreet needn't be disclosed, however, be aware that tattoos may be visible under a shirt or a blouse, and this too is unacceptable.

If you do have visible tattoos, the natural instinct is to camouflage them with cosmetics. Unfortunately, this will be insufficient and may cause you to be dismissed later on. All crew will be required to sign a disclosure that they bear no visible tattoos, therefore, if a tattoo is discovered during the medical examination in Dubai, you will be sent home. The best option is to have the tattoo laser removed.

Piercings

Facial piercings and multiple ear piercings are unacceptable. Remove the piercings before the interview and do your best to conceal the holes if they appear obvious or unsightly.

Braces

Braces are an unknown and unexpected cause for elimination. Temporary braces that are barely noticeable and can be removed are generally permissible, however, you should remove them for the interview to avoid being unfairly eliminated. Unfortunately, those of you with permanent silver tracks, and even the modern invisible braces, will be eliminated, so you should consider waiting for the braces to be removed before you apply.

Style Guide:

LADIES

 Consider: Style

Presence is achieved when you look and feel good, so it is important to wear an outfit that you feel the most confident and powerful in. However, in order to stand out for the right reasons, it is important to achieve balance: Balance between how the outfit makes you feel and what impression it creates.

Your outfit should be thoughtful and demonstrate that you have made an effort. So buy the best quality garnets that you can afford, and be sure they are clean and neatly pressed. The idea is to look business-like, yet stylish.

Emirates are a very conservative and classy airline, and you will be better perceived if you wear classic business attire. Tasteful, elegant and sophisticated are good objectives to aim for, and you'll want to avoid appearing flashy or overly sexy. Well-coordinated and tailored separates achieve this perfectly, as does a fitted dress in a conservative style: Conservative implying a modest neckline and appropriate length. Always opt for a skirt over pants, as this will create a feminine and streamlined appearance and match any ensemble with a quality tailored jacket. This is a powerful piece that can tie a look together and create a wonderfully professional appearance.

Avoid heavy patterns, as these can appear overwhelming, and be sure to select wrinkle resistant fabrics, such as wool. Nothing looks more unprofessional or unprepared than rumpled clothes or wrinkled shirts.

Consider: Colour

Colour is a powerful tool that can dramatically increase your chances of standing out. Used appropriately, colour will help you to convey confidence, express your personality and enhance your complexion. So, consider adding a splash of your favourite colour to your outfit for added pizazz.

If you choose to wear a bold piece, be sure that you have the courage of your convictions because you will certainly be noticed and expectations will be set much higher. You wouldn't want to be noticed for looking extremely uncomfortable or for looking washed out by an unflattering colour.

You don't need to be draped in colour to make an impact. In fact, the safest way to wear colour is to add subtle splashes through your accessories, accents or pop pieces. Subtle accents can bring out the sparkle in your eyes and liven up your outfit, without appearing overwhelming or degrading your professionalism.

Whichever option you choose, it is important to avoid wearing the same colour combination as the Emriates uniform, as this will appear that you trying too hard. Instead, opt for subtle splashes of red or beige in your accessories and pop pieces. More on this later.

Consider: Shoes

The benefits of wearing heels are obvious. They make your legs look longer, shapelier and more feminine, so it is a good idea to wear them if you feel comfortable to do so. Killer heels may have the added butt lifting effect, however, this is not the look you want to achieve at the Emirates interview. Heels should be no higher than 3" and thin soles will appear more professional and elegant than thick platforms.

For those of you who are not used to wearing heels or are on the taller side, 1" inch heels will still provide the benefits of wearing heels without the excess height. Give them a try, and be sure to have lots of practice before the big day.

Only wear shoes which are clean and in good condition. Tatty shoes, with scuffed toes or heels will detract from the polished image you are trying to create. Court shoes will appear more professional and polished than open toes and sling backs, and splashes of colour are perfectly acceptable as long as they are tasteful and not overly sexy or decorative fashion styles. Remember, tasteful, elegant and sophisticated.

Consider: Hosiery

If wearing a dress or a skirt, pantyhose in plain nude or black are essential for creating a polished and professional image, as they will ensure your legs look perfectly smooth and blemish free. Be sure to select a good quality pair, as they will hug your curves better than cheaper alternatives and will be less likely to create the unsightly wrinkled effect around the knees and ankles. Be sure to spot check them before the interview to ensure that there are no runs or ladders and always have an emergency pair in your handbag for good measure.

 ## Consider: Accessories

Jewellery is a great way to spice up a boring black ensemble, giving it character and pizazz, however, be sure to keep your pieces minimal and conservative. Wear no more than one ring per hand, and one set of earrings, and avoid oversized fashion pieces. Bangles that clink can become distracting and annoying, so it is best to avoid them. A timepiece can be worn, but be sure the style is appropriate and turn off any audible sounds.

Observe caution when wearing an engagement ring or wedding band, as such pieces will draw attention to your private life and will leave you open to discrimination.

Consider: Grooming

Grooming is an essential aspect when presenting a polished image. They are the finishing touches that tie your appearance together. Bitten nails, unsightly blemishes and scruffy hair can undermine even the very best of outfits. So be sure to pay extra special attention to the following areas:

Nails should be clean, neatly trimmed and reasonable in length. Nail polish should match in colour and it is best to avoid charms, glitter and multi-coloured polish.

Use cosmetics to conceal blemishes and enhance your assets, but avoid going over the top. Tastefully applied makeup is the best way to achieve a polished and sophisticated look. A touch of mascara and some eyeliner paired with a dash of lipstick is all that is needed. Remember, you are attending an interview not going out for a night on the town. Refined elegance will work better than dramatic.

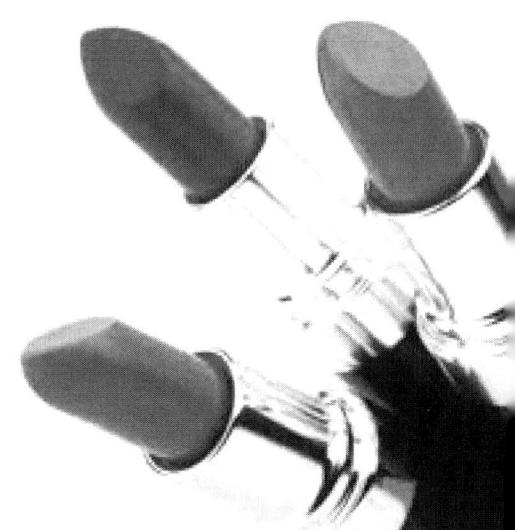

Tip: Red lipstick is part of the Emirates uniform, so wearing it to the interview is a fantastic psychological finishing touch. Be sure to visit a cosmetics counter to find the ideal shade of red for your complexion. The wrong shade will be noticeable, as it will wash you out and ruin the effect. Wearing your hair in a neat bun will also work towards achiving an impact.

Hair should be neat and well groomed, and outrageous colours or styles should be avoided. Frizzy or loose ends can appear messy so brush and fix them into place if necessary. Freshly trimmed hair will be easier to style and keep looking fresh, so book into the salon if necessary.

If you choose to wear perfume, select a light scent and wear it sparingly. There is nothing more off-putting than an overpowering odour, even a pleasant one.

Visible tattoos and facial piercings are not acceptable. Tattoos will need to be concealed and piercings removed. That applies to multiple earrings too.

Consider: The ultimate advantage

Interviewers need to be able to visualise you in the position, so the very act of looking like you are already Emirates cabin crew will create a great psychological advantage.

Now, I am not implying that you find a suit in a matching colour to the Emirates' uniform with hat and scarf to match. Sure this would make you stand out, but not for the right reasons. Subtlety is the key to success with this strategy. You're trying to capture the airlines aesthetic appeal, not look like you are attending a fancy dress parade.

The best way to pull this off is to look at the cabin crew who already work for Emirates. Injecting a splash of the corporate colour into your accessories is a great touch. Another is to tend to your grooming in the same way you would if offered the position.

The effort you put in to this will show and it will be apparent that you have done your research to understand the airline's culture. The psychological impact this one trick can achieve is astonishing and should not be underestimated.

Avoid: Fashion faux pas

If you would like to be taken seriously, you need to avoid the following fatal mistakes.

1. Push up bra and plunging necklines

2. Bare midriff

3. Too much makeup or hair product

4. Unnecessary accessories

5. Wrinkled or unkempt clothes

6. Ill fitting garments

7. Cheap and translucent blouses

8. Scuffed or tatty shoes

9. Short skirt

10. Extremely high heels or large platforms

11. Bitten or over the top nails

12. Strong perfume

Style Guide:
GENTS

When it comes to looking professional, the options for gents are no doubt limited. Formal business attire is essential for creating a professional, polished and streamlined look, however, when every other male candidate is also wearing business attire, how do you stand out from the crowd? It is the attention you pay to the finer details that will show that you have made an effort, and it is this that will get you noticed.

Consider: Fit & Quality

The key to looking your best in a suit is to pay special attention to fit and quality. A well-tailored suit, in a wrinkle free fabric, will create a polished and professional look that will surely set you apart from the rest. Off the rack suits are a popular choice because they are convenient and inexpensive, however, a ready to wear suit is often the worst option when making a good impression is your top priority. As such, it is advisable to purchase the best quality suit you can afford. A custom tailored suit is the obvious choice, however if finances will not stretch to this, purchase an off the rack suit and have some tailored alterations carried out for an inexpensive alternative.

Whichever option you choose, be sure to pay attention to selecting a good quality fabric. Natural fabrics are far better than synthetic fabrics or blends. In particular, wool, such as merino, cashmere and angora, will offer the best in comfort, wrinkle resistance, and longevity.

Consider: Shirt

A good quality, 100% cotton shirt, with long sleeves is essential for appearing professional and crisp. White, ecru and blue are classic and conservative choices and should be your first choice.

Dark shirts are somewhat taboo as they are often considered a style choice, rather than a professional one. As such, you need to proceed with caution if this is what you feel most comfortable wearing. On the one hand it is important to wear what you feel confident and powerful in, but on the other, it is important to achieve balance: Balance between how the outfit makes you feel and what impression it creates. Airlines are no doubt much more open to personal style choices, however, it is a choice that may not be viewed favourably, no matter how powerful and confident it makes you feel. Therefore, it is far better to play it safe.

When it comes to choosing a collar, remember that it will frame your face. As such, you will want to select a collar that brings balance to your face shape. A wide spread collar will compliment a thin and long face well, while a classic point works better on a round face.

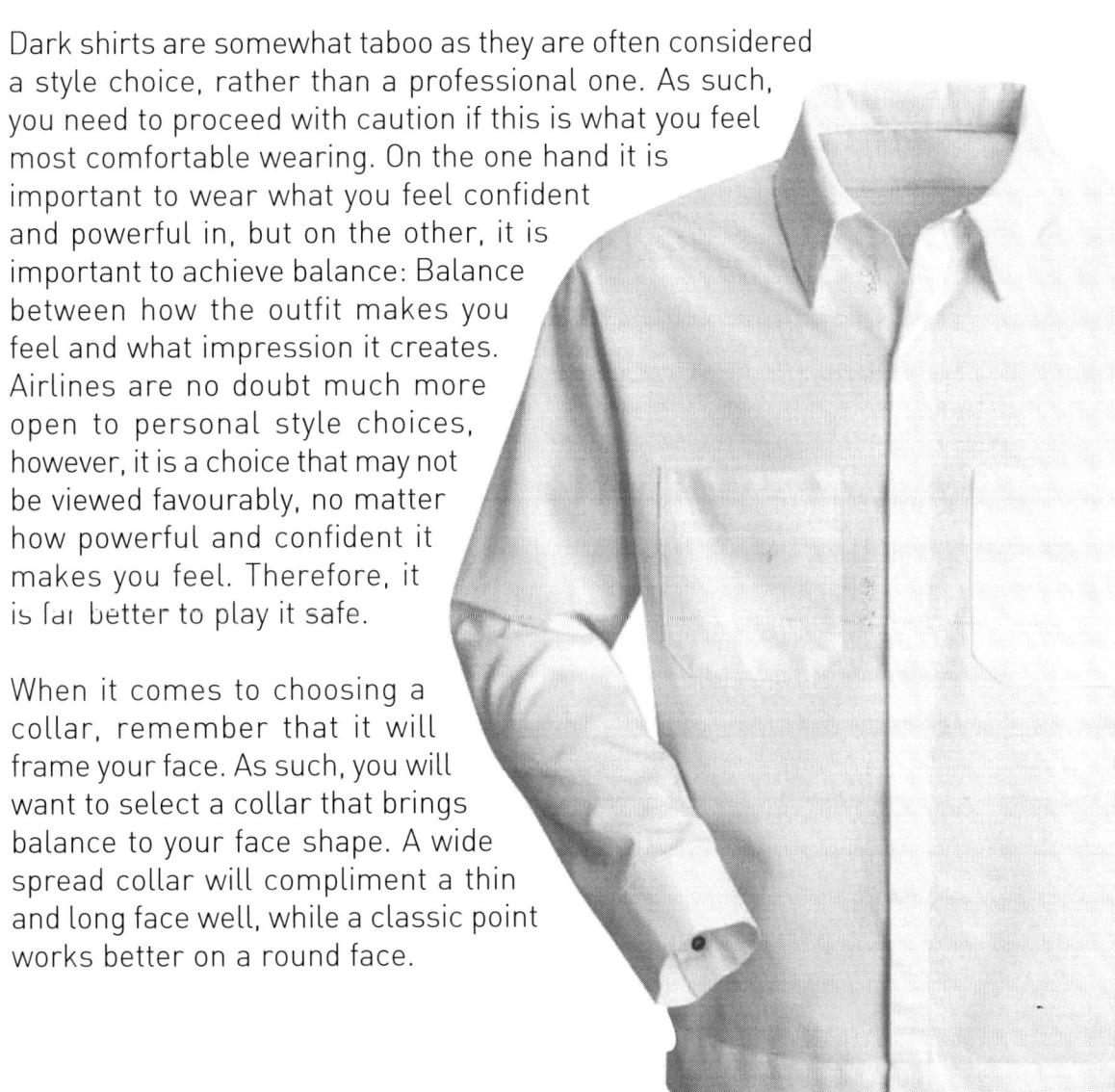

⚠ Consider: Pattern & Colour

With regards to colour and pattern, it is best to err on the side of caution. Traditional colours, such as navy blue or charcoal grey, are great alternatives to the standard black, while brown, beige and taupe will appear too casual. If you do decide to wear black, try opting for a subtle pinstripe pattern to break up the monotony and strength of the colour.

⚠ Consider: Tie

The tie is an extremely important accessory, as it is often the first thing that a person notices.

Since it frames your face, it is important to consider the colour choice carefully because the wrong colour can suck the sparkle out of your complexion, leaving you looking dull and lifeless. When considering colour, assess how it interacts and enhances your complexion. Does red make your skin look bright, vibrant and well rested? or does it make you look sallow and washed out? Likewise, does blue bring a sparkle to your eyes, or does it make your complexion look muddy and ashen?

Pattern is another factor that needs consideration. Character ties and exotic patterns, while demonstrating personality, are not the ideal interview choice. Instead, opt for subtle stripes, simple designs or block colours for a classic and professional look.

For a strong and confident appeal opt for a larger knot, such as the Pratt or Windsor and aim for a length that falls to the same level as the belt buckle. Tie bars and clips may also be worn to keep the tie in place.

Consider: Shoes & Socks

Shoes should be worn in a style and colour that coordinates with the overall look of your suit. Lace up shoes are the classic and safe option, however, loafers can also be worn if they are suitable. A thin sole will create a more professional image than thick rubber soles.

Nicked heels and scruffy toes will ruin the whole outfit, so invest in a new pair if necessary and never underestimate the importance of a good shoeshine.

Socks should be inconspicuous so they don't draw any attention. As such, they should be dark in colour and long enough to cover your calves so that your flesh is not exposed when seated.

Consider: Accessories

Accessories are finishing touches and should be treated as such. This means that they should remain simple to complement your outfit. Cufflinks may be worn if you are wearing a buttonless shirt, and a leather belt with an understated buckle ought not be forgotten.

While a leather briefcase is unnecessary, a leather portfolio will look much more professional than carrying lots of loose papers.

When it comes to jewellery, the simpler and less of it, the better. One ring and a tasteful wristwatch is all that is necessary to project a professional image.

Consider: Grooming

When it comes to grooming a good haircut and clean-shaven face are essential. A few days prior to the interview, have your hair freshly cut or trimmed and be sure to shave on the morning of the interview. Be careful not to cut yourself and try to prevent razor burn.

Nails are another aspect that is often neglected and underestimated by male candidates. A manicure is an attention to detail that will be noticed and appreciated, so visit a manicurist a few days before the interview.

If you must wear cologne, be sure not to use too much as it can be distracting and suffocating.

Consider: The Ultimate Advantage

Interviewers need to be able to visualise you in the position, so the very act of looking like you are already cabin crew will create a great psychological advantage. Now, I am not implying that you arrive in something too similar to the Emirates' uniform; however, it doesn't hurt to capture an element of the industries aesthetic appeal. The one item that captures this look the best is a fitted waistcoat. It is an element often under-utilised, but its stylish appeal works wonders within the airline industry.

Some of you may baulk at this idea, however, it is an element, which will get you noticed. Not only do they create a business-like and streamlined appearance, but it will show that you have made an extra special effort. Take a look at the Virgin Atlantic uniform to get a sense of its style for yourself. If a waistcoat does fit in with your personal style, consider including it in your repertoire.

Avoid: Fashion Faux Pas

If you would like to be taken seriously, you need to avoid the following fatal mistakes.

1. Short sleeves

2. Strong cologne

3. Too much hair product

4. Excessive jewellery

5. Wrinkled or unkempt clothes

6. Ill fitting garments

7. Scuffed or tatty shoes

8. Visible tattoos or piercings

9. Rubber sports watch

10. Bow tie or suspenders

11. Excessive facial hair

In Conclusion

While the advice and guidance given in this chapter may sound obvious, unnecessary and, even, unimportant, it has been my experience that many candidates fail to create an impression because they are either confused or uninformed about the standard of dress expected of them or because they neglect to pay enough attention to the details.

Following this guidance will not only multiply your chances of attracting the interviewers attention, but you will also stand out for having made an extra effort.

In the grand scheme of things, it does not matter how well you are dressed or how much effort you have gone through if the rest of your delivery is poor. So, continue reading and you will discover important steps that will make you truly memorable.

CREATE THE
RIGHT
IMPRESSION

Consider

YOUR COMMUNICATION

Because effective communication skills are essential for interview success, it is important to be mindful of how your communication is received. This means that you must consider not only the words you use, but also how your tonality and body language complement or contradict those words.

Consider the following communication guidelines:

Word choice

Words are important because they communicate and convey your message succinctly. So, even at a low 7% accountability, your word choice can mean the difference between a powerful, captivating and influential exchange, and a weak, disempowering and ineffective one.

Action words

Action words are positive, powerful and directive, and should be used abundantly. Action words include: Communicated, conveyed, directed, listened, persuaded, arranged, handled and improved.

Filler words

Filler words are useless and annoying verbal mannerisms such as "you know," "huh," "erm," "kind of," "ummm," and "uh". Besides sounding unprofessional, they also distract attention from the message. Filler words should be avoided at all costs.

Undermining words

Words and phrases such as 'I think,' 'I hope,' 'maybe,' 'sort of,' 'perhaps,' 'I guess,' all undermine your message and credibility by creating the impression that you don't trust your own knowledge or opinion. Eliminating these phrases will drastically improve the quality of any message.

Jargon, slang and cliches

Specialist terminology and informal expressions can confuse an outside audience. Avoid these where possible, and stick to simple, clear and coherent language.

Vocal quality

Tonality plays a key role in sending the correct messages. So, if your aim is to project confidence, enthusiasm and expertise, it is important to exercise control and awareness of your tonality throughout your interactions.

Pitch

Pitch refers to the degree of highness and lowness in your voice. A variation in your pitch creates meaning, adds clarity and makes what you are saying more interesting. For instance: A rise in your pitch suggests you are asking a question, which indicates doubt, uncertainty and hesitation. A fall in pitch indicates a statement, which suggests certainty and assurance.

Tempo

Tempo refers to the speed of your voice. If you speak too slowly, you risk losing the interest and attention of your audience. If you speak too fast, others may find you difficult to follow. The key is to maintain a pace, which is fast enough to maintain interest, yet slow enough to be clear.

Volume

Speaking in a loud volume suggests aggression, while a quiet volume indicates shyness and makes it difficult to be heard. The key to determining the appropriate volume is to keep your voice loud enough to be heard, but soft enough to be clear. Modulation of volume can also be introduced to keep your speech interesting and add extra emphasis.

Articulation

Articulation refers to vocal clarity. Regardless of our pitch, tempo, volume and accent, you need to make a conscious effort to enunciate clearly.

Communication Barriers

Barriers to effective communication may arise for a number of reasons. When these barriers do occur, you are forced to become even more effective in your ability to communicate. The strategies below will help overcome some of these more effectively.

 ## Language

If you struggle with the native language of the airline, or have a very strong accent, speak slowly and clearly, ask for clarification and check for understanding, avoid idioms and jargon, use gestures and be specific, listen actively and be patient.

 ## Cultural

Because every culture has its own set of values, beliefs and behaviours, the potential for confusion and misunderstanding is high. Even when we speak the same language, these differences can lead to challenges. To effectively connect with an individual from a culturally different background, it is important to be sensitive and respectful, avoid prejudice and stereotyping, and be aware of using questionable language and gestures.

Gender

Barriers in communication between genders exist primarily because men and women have different communication patterns. To overcome these barriers, it is important to appreciate, learn and understand the different strengths and styles that exist.

While men tend to be more direct and factual, women tend to be indirect and tactful. Men have a preference for reason and logic, are competitive and are interested in power, rank and status. Women are empathetic and feeling oriented. They value relationships and like to build rapport. Men communicate to exchange information and solve problems, while women communicate to share and a build connection.

Emotional

Emotional barriers within an interview situation manifest themselves through fear, shyness or restraint. When we feel distracted by these emotional states, our ability to communicate at an effective level is severely inhibited. We may wrongly interpret the actions and words of others, and may not effectively express our own opinion. We may even stop listening to the other person as our internal dialogue takes over.

To effectively deal with these barriers, it is important to treat the underlying cause of such emotions.

Let your body

DO THE TALKING

The way you carry yourself, the gestures you use and your facial expressions communicate all sorts of messages. If you appear to lack confidence, seem evasive, or exhibit negative body language it is only natural that the interviewer will want to dig further to find out why your body is contradicting your words. So it is worth learning to control certain aspects so that you can convey the message of a well-balanced, confident individual.

The reason why your body language is so important is that it supports and reinforces what you say. In essence you appear to be exactly what you say you are.

Gestures

We use open gestures when we are feeling confident and relaxed, and are being honest and sincere, therefore, keep your arms unfolded, your legs uncrossed and your palms open. Sitting or standing with your arms crossed will be interpreted as a defensive posture and will give the impression that you are uncomfortable, bored, or have something to hide. Likewise, standing in your hands in your pockets suggests unease.

Touching your nose during the interview is commonly interpreted as an indication of dishonesty, so even if it itches, it is best to grin and bear it. Observe caution if you experience the tendency to rub your neck as this too can be misinterpreted as boredom or unease.

Gesturing can be useful for adding emphasis to what you are saying and, if the movements you employ are subtle and controlled, it is perfectly okay to use gestures to express yourself and endorse your words. For best results, keep any movements below shoulder level, but above the waistline.

Posture

Posture is fundamental to appearing alert, confident and motivated, and yet it is shocking to see how many candidates forget this one simple rule. Take a look around the room next time you attend a group interview and you will see candidates slouching and generally looking bored and inattentive while they wait to be assessed.

I understand that the wait can be long and tiresome, however, it is important that you do not let this happen to you. This is the period when you are being watched very closely and letting your posture relax too much will demonstrate disrespect and give the impression that you lack interest.

To portray the image of a confident and motivated person, adopt an upright and attentive posture that is open, yet relaxed. Keep your chin parallel to the floor, shoulders back and spine straight.

If seated, lean slightly forward with your hands loosely in your lap, or on the table. Place both feet flat on the floor, or cross your ankles. And always be sure to direct your body and your feet towards the interviewer and not at the door, as this will give the impression that you feel uncomfortable and are ready to flee.

If standing, keep your arms loosely at your side or behind your back and plant your feet about 8-10 inches apart. If standing for long periods, place one foot slightly in front of the other to allow you to smoothly and unnoticeably shift weight between your feet.

Your carriage

The way you carry yourself is a powerful indicator of how you feel. To be perceived as confident and professional, walk briskly with an erect posture. Keep your shoulders back, your arms loosely at your side, and chin parallel to the floor.

Facial expressions

Your facial expressions convey a wide range of attitudes, feelings and emotions, and these can have a significant impact on your ability to connect with others. Because of this, it is important to be aware of the story your face is telling and work to convey an attentive, sincere and interested expression.

A positive expression can certainly include a smile, but doesn't necessarily imply its inclusion. In fact, maintaining a constant smile is not only uncomfortable, but it is also completely unnecessary. Instead, an open expression that includes a gentle and understated smile, soft eyes and slightly elevated eyebrows will result in a soft and pleasant expression.

Large smiles should be reserved for introductions and the occasional injection during conversation.

Handshake

Your handshake says a lot about you. A firm handshake conveys confidence, assertiveness and professionalism while a weak, limp handshake suggests shyness and insecurity. A strong, crushing handshake indicates aggression and dominance, and should be avoided.

To perform a professional and confident handshake, follow these simple guidelines:

Before connecting for the handshake establish eye contact, smile and lean slightly forward. As you extend your right hand, keep your hand straight and thumb pointing upwards. When your hands connect engage a firm, but not crushing, grip. Pump one to three times, for a duration of 1-3 seconds, and break away.

The Eyes

DEFINITELY HAVE IT

Good eye contact is one of the most important factors of body language. Shifty eyes, or complete avoidance of contact can suggest dishonesty, boredom, rudeness, insecurity or shyness.

If you find eye contact anxiety provoking and uncomfortable, direct your gaze at their eyebrows, forehead, or bridge of the nose. This is not a permanent solution by any means, but it will certainly ease you into the process.

In an attempt to forge eye contact, be aware not to stare as this can indicate aggression and make others feel uncomfortable. To avoid this extreme, lighten your gaze and keep it friendly. This can be achieved by allowing your eyes to go slightly out of focus.

If you have notes, you can temporarily break eye contact as you refer to these, and if there is a second recruitment officer present, this will give you opportunity to break eye contact as you periodically direct your focus back and forth between the two.

Aim to maintain eye contact for 80-90% of the time.

Caution:

SMOKERS

Due to the non-smoking environment on board an aircraft and the fact that you will not be able to step outside for a quickie mid-fligh, smokers will be viewed unfavourably. So if you are partial to a cigarette or two, it is important that you refrain from 'sparking up' at any time before or during the interview, as the smell of smoke will linger on your clothing. Once the interview is over, you may of course have one, but be sure you are well away from the building.

To avoid your interview garments becoming infested by the smell of stale smoke, have your outfit cleaned thoroughly and then keep it zipped up in a suit bag away from your smoking environment. On the day of your interview, be sure to wash thoroughly before you handle it.

Although it is possible to try to conceal the smell of smoke, the effort required and the risks involved are far too great and it simply isn't worth it. The best course of action on the day of the interview is to wear a nicotine patch.

If you find the thought of not smoking for the day too much to bear, temporarily switch over to e-cigarettes, but be sure to use it only within the privacy of the W.C. and never in public view.

So, what should you say if you are asked whether you smoke? Well, this will depend on you. You can of course say no, you could be tactful with the truth and simply state that you have recently given up or you can respond in the affirmative. Whichever answer you choose is your decision, but beware that being honest in this instance may be the quickest way for your resume to hit the rejection pile.

If you are looking to make cabin crew your future career, it is worthwhile considering kicking the addiction in the long term.

CREATE A
MEMORABLE
IMPRESSION

Create a
MEMORABLE IMPRESSION

When faced with hundreds, and possibly thousands, of other candidates, merely creating a good impression just isn't enough. You need to be memorable. The trouble is, very few people know how to truly differentiate themselves from the competition. Most candidates enter the interview in their own little bubble, thinking that they only need to dress well and sell their skills and experience. Unfortunately, this is only a small part of it.

Creating a memorable impression goes far beyond what you wear and how you carry yourself, and even beyond the skills and experience you posses. In fact, it is so rare that only 2% of candidates ever make it through to being hired.

The secret to creating a memorable impression will surprise you in its simplicity, and yet many candidates are unaware that such an advantage even exists, let alone know how to evoke it. They often enter the process only prepared for the hard sell, if they are prepared at all, and end up merely blending in with the rest of the crowd.

Recruiters see this same thing time and time again, so any candidate who is prepared to put in just that little bit of extra effort will naturally stand out, and it is these candidates who, ultimately, get hired.

So what is this mysterious phenomenon and how can you use it to your advantage?

The Art

OF THE CONNECTION

This technique is actually not mysterious at all. In fact, it is not even a secret. The technique involves creating a connection or, most commonly referred to as, establishing a rapport. Rapport is such a powerful tool, as it is the quickest way to achieve a sensation of familiarity and trust between you and the recruiter. It is so powerful, in fact, that it can even sway the hiring decision in your favour.

Why does this technique work so well? Have you ever met someone for the first time and yet you felt a strong connection, just as if you'd known him or her forever? This is rapport in action. If you can establish this level of rapport with the recruiter or undercover officers, you can be sure they will remember you favourably.

The quickest and easiest way to achieve a connection this strong is through the act of mirroring.

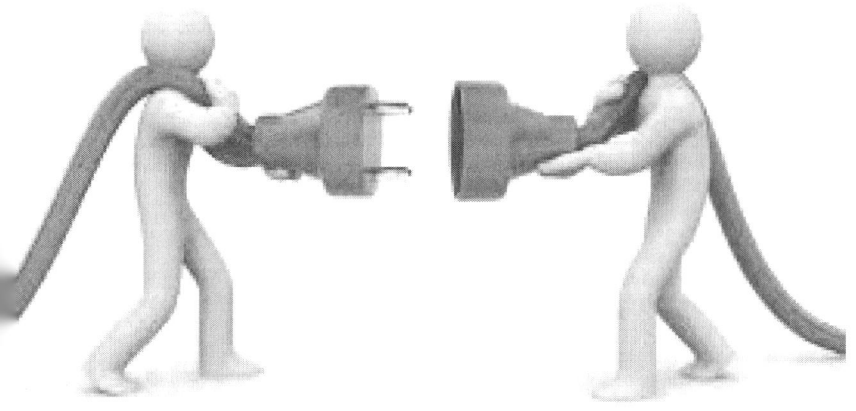

Mirror, Mirror

Mirroring is a process whereby you match your communication style, posture and mannerisms to those of another person. It is something you do naturally when you are deep in rapport with another person and is created by a deep feeling of unity. Using it consciously can evoke the sensation that the two of you are very much in sync just as readily as if it had occurred at a subconscious level, only you can be in control and use it to your own advantage.

As a note of caution, mirroring is something that must be done subtly to be effective. As such, it is important not to match every movement and not to react instantly to every change, else your motives will become obvious and the effectiveness of the technique will be lost.

For seamless results, take note of the following guidelines.

Body Language

As you are speaking with the recruiter, make a mental note of how they are sitting or standing, and what they are doing with their hands. Then, subtly mirror their position and gestures. If they are leaning forward, you might lean forward also. If they have their hands clasped on the table, you might do the same.

The best time to mirror a position is when you engage in dialogue. For example: The recruiter leans forward as he or she begins to ask you a question. As you engage in your follow up response, a change in position would appear natural and go completely unnoticed.

Be cautious not to mirror any closed signals, such as crossing your arms, as this will only accomplish a negative connection.

Communication Style

Mirroring a communication style can be done through using similar words or phrases, matching the sensory style, or mimicking the pitch, tempo and volume of their voice.

Words and Phrases
You can make a fantastic psychological impact simply by injecting the recruiter's own terminology and sequence of words into your answers. For example, if the interviewer points out that they are looking for and value a candidate who is 'team spirited', inject the same phrase into your answer. Simply stating that "I work well in a team", or "I am a team player", while implying the same values, will not create the same strong psychological impact as using the interviewers own words.

Pitch, Tempo and Volume

Matching your pitch, tempo and volume to the recruiters speaking style will make you appear in tune to what they are saying. This will speed up the rapport process and greatly improve your chances of creating a favourable impression. Keep pace with the interviewer and assess their basic conversational style. If they have a fast pace, assume the same characteristics. If they are analytical and introspective, slow down your responses to their speed.

Sensory Style

While we all use a mix of the sensory styles: Visual, kinaesthetic and auditory, we tend to have a dominant style that we gravitate towards. If, during the course of the interview, it becomes obvious that the recruiter has a preference towards a particular sensory style, you can adjust your style accordingly to establish a deeper connection.

Visual people use words that reflect their visual style, such as: 'I <u>see</u> what you mean', 'It <u>looks</u> to me like...', 'I <u>imagine</u> that...'

Auditory people use hearing words, such as: 'I <u>hear</u> what you are saying', 'We'll <u>discuss</u> this further', 'I <u>hear</u> you loud and clear'

Kinaesthetic people use action words, such as: 'It <u>feels</u> as if...', 'It <u>slipped</u> my mind', 'I have a solid <u>grasp</u>...'

Next time you are in a public place, observe how people who appear to be closely connected do these same things. You could even try this out for yourself next time you are out for lunch with a close friend or family member. In fact, because this technique can appear uncomfortable and awkward the first time you try it, practicing will, in time, make it almost natural and automatic, and you may even find that your relationships begin to blossom more than usual.

Leading

Leading is an influencing technique that can be used to judge the level of connection. For example: If you feel you have achieved rapport with the recruiter, you could change position or make a gesture to see If the recruiter follows your lead. If this does occur, you can be sure that you have established a strong connection. It the test reveals that the connection is not as strong as you thought, simply go back to mirroring to re-establish and strengthen the connection.

Disconnection

It is important to be perceptive to signs that the recruiter has become disconnected so that you can be proactive in re-establishing the connection.

Before attempting to reconnect, however, it is important to establish the accuracy of your perceptions because you may have simply misread the signal or it could be a by-product of a paranoid imagination. Similarly, the perceived signal may be a momentary motion that has no substance or it may be unrelated to you entirely.

To reliably determine the accuracy of your observation, you first need to scan for clusters of signals that are supportive of your perception. If you observe two or more congruent signals, this is a definite cluster. Next, you can test our connection by attempting to 'lead' (see above). If the recruiter doesn't follow, this is also a sure sign that a disconnection has taken place.

When to use it

During the group stages, you will not have an opportunity to forge any kind of connection with the official recruiters, however, you will be up close and very personal with the undercover team and it is here that you will be focusing much of your attention during these early stages.

The trouble is, how do you know who is undercover and who is a candidate? Unfortunately ,you don't. As such, the only possible way to accomplish this task is to make this same effort with every candidate you meet. While this may seem like an arduous and inefficient task, your efforts will pay off many times over, as you will gain an advantage like no other. In the worst instance, you will come away with a few new friends.

During the latter stages of the final interview, you can refocus your efforts on the official recruiters. This is where the technique will really come into its own and you can use it to its full advantage.

The one type
WHO ALWAYS GETS THE JOB OFFER

As you can now see, there is always one type who gets the job offer, but it isn't the best looking one as myths and legend would have you believe. The simple truth is that recruiters hire those individuals that they personally like and feel a connection with.

The biggest mistake most candidates make is that they enter the interview focused only on themselves and miss any opportunity to make a connection. A candidate who makes an effort will not only come across as more genuine and sincere, they will also instantly differentiate themselves from the competition, so it is certainly worthwhile putting the extra effort into perfecting this technique.

Just like

OLD FRIENDS

Another trick, which can be used as an adjunct to the previous technique, is to think of the recruiter as a good friend. Now I am not suggesting you take this literally, or you risk appearing too informal and familiar, what I am suggesting is that you enter the interview in a natural and conversational frame of mind.

The point of this technique is to help you relax, but also to assist the interviewer in breaking the ice. Simply initiating some friendly dialogue as you first meet the recruiter will help you to create an aura of a warm and approachable person, but also one who is relaxed and confident. Such a personable approach can help the interviewer feel more comfortable in your presence and will certainly get the interview off to a great start.

Naturally you will want to use common sense here to avoid stepping over the invisible line, however, it is important to remember that most candidates will only be thinking about themselves. The interviewer will appreciate your effort to connect.

The enthusiastic
APPROACH

If there is just one more thing that can set one candidate apart from the rest, it is the expression of a sincere passion and enthusiasm for the job, airline and the opportunity. Sadly, many people believe that showing enthusiasm will be mistaken for desperation and, as such, suppress their enthusiasm in favour of the laid back and relaxed approach. The truth is, the laid back approach is often mistaken for indifference or disinterest, and this can severely hinder your chances of success.

Another misconception is that being enthusiastic means that you need to be loaded with energy and bouncing off the walls. This is bordering on excitement, rather than enthusiasm, and is not ideal either. As discussed previously, the idea is to match the tempo of the person you are speaking to, and injecting too much energy can make it difficult for others to relate and connect with you, not to mention exhausting. You can certainly be calm and still be enthusiastic.

So what exactly is enthusiasm and how can you use it appropriately?

Use it appropriately

There are several ways that you can display your enthusiasm. This could be through an eagerness and willingness to learn, your facial expression and smile, an expression of pride in your work, actively listening and asking questions, taking notes and even through your knowledge and research about the opportunity and the airline.

You can also be upfront about your enthusiasm by stating it directly. For instance, when asked "Why do you want to be cabin crew?", speak from the heart as you tell them your personal story and the steps you have been taking to achieve your dream. If you have a sincere passion for meeting people from different cultures, express it. If you have a genuine love for assisting in the comfort of others, use it. If you have been participating in volunteer work to enhance your skills for the position, tell them. This is truly where you will stand head over heels above the run-of-the-mill answers that they hear 95% of the time.

Don't underestimate the power

It sounds simple, and even, superfluous, when compared to tangible skills and experiences, however, do not underestimate the power of honest and sincere enthusiasm. It is contagious and will energise those around you. More importantly, recruiters will pick up on your positive energy and will sense that you will approach the job with vigour.

Make an effort

TO USE THE RECRUITER'S NAME

When attending an interview of any kind, the most important people in attendance are the recruitment personnel, and yet, most candidates enter the process and make no effort to remember, acknowledge or even use the recruiter's name. They are so wrapped up in their own selves, that they view the officer as simply an obstacle or obstruction in the way of them achieving their dream job.

Using a person's name in conversation is the quickest and easiest way to forge a connection. This is especially true in an interview situation when 95% of candidates will never take such initiative. Use it during the resume handover or mini interview and see the reaction for yourself. It is a simple strategy that will gain you instant recognition and make you stand out from the crowd.

STAND OUT AS AN
INFORMED
CANDIDATE

The following pages contain some basic facts about Emirates to get you started, however, Emirates may have introduced new routes, earned more awards and have alternative plans for the future since the time of printing. It is therefore advisable that you check the internet for any new and updated information. Visit the Emirates web site at www.emirates.com, read company literature and press releases.

Preliminary

RESEARCH

Taking the time to conduct research about Emirates will enable you to ask intelligent questions, as well as answer any that are posed. Your informed knowledge will give a positive impression about you and your motivation to work for Emirates, thus giving you a competitive edge over less informed candidates.

If you know nothing about the airline other than the colour of the uniform, the salary and their best destinations, you certainly won't create a positive impression.

There is no need to know the whole history, but you should at least know some basic information, such as:

- What is their route network?
- Are there any future plans for expansion or growth?
- Where is their base airport located?
- Who are the airline's major competitors?
- Who are the key people within Emirates?
- What do you like about Emirates?
- How long have they been operating?
- What are some of the awards they have won?
- Why do you want to work for Emirates, rather than another airline?

Historical

OVERVIEW

Emirates Airline (EK) is the international airline of the United Arab Emirates, based in Dubai.

Since beginning its operations in October of 1985, the airline has experienced extraordinary growth to become one of the world's most prestigious international airlines. The airline currently boasts an astonishing 300+ international awards and is among the world's most profitable airlines and among the ten largest.

Emirates started out as a regional carrier with just two leased aircraft, serving only 3 destinations -Bombay, Delhi and Karachi. Within its first two years of operation, Emirates had acquired three fully owned aircraft (a Boeing 727 and two Airbus A310-300's) and had expanded its network to include 6 new destinations (Dhaka, Colombo, Cairo, Oman, London, Istanbul and Frankfurt). The airline now operates more than 220 aircraft, serving over 140 destinations in more than 80 countries on six continents.

During the 2013/14 financial year, Emirates carried 44.5 million passengers, and this number is set to rise as the airline has orders for over 300 additional craft of their books.

Key Facts

(From Wikipedia)

IATA airline designation:	EK
ICAO airline designation:	UAE
Callsign:	Emirates
Founded:	1985
Commenced operations:	25th October 1985
Hub:	Dubai International Airport
Frequent flyer program:	Skywards
Airport lounge:	Emirates lounge
Subsidiaries:	Arabian Adventures
	Congress Solutions International
	Emirates Holidays
	Emirates Tours
Fleet sizc	231
Destinations:	142
Company slogan:	Fly Emirates
Parent company:	The Emirates Group
Headquarters:	Garhoud, Dubai, United Arab Emirates
Key people:	Ahmed bin Saeed Al Maktoum (Chairman and CEO)
	Tim Clark (President)
	Maurice Flanagan (Executive Vice Chairman)

Awards
FOR EXCELLENCE

Emirates has received an extensive range of awards and commendations for every kind of service that they provide. The list is too long to include in this book, however, I have inlcuded a selection of the most signficant below. More information can be found on their website at www.emirates.com

2014

Aviation Industry Awards
Emirates named Aviation Company of the Year

Aviation Industry Awards
Emirates wins Aircraft Operator Award

Business Traveller (ME) awards
Emirates named Best Airline Worldwide

Business Traveller (ME) awards
Emirates named Airline with the Best First Class

Business Traveller (ME) awards
Emirates named Airline with the Best Business Class

Business Traveller (ME) awards
Emirates named Airline with the Best Cabin Staff

2013

2013 CondÈ Nast Middle East Traveller Readersí Choice Awards
Emirates named 'Best Airline – Business'

2013 CondÈ Nast Middle East Traveller Readersí Choice Awards
Emirates named 'Best Airline – Leisure'

2013 Airline Passenger Experience (APEX) Passenger Choice Awards
Emirates named Best in the Middle East

Future Travel Experience (FTE) Awards
Emirates wins Best Up in the Air Experience award

The Gulf Business Industry Awards 2013
Emirates honoured as Aviation Company of the Year

CondÈ Nast Travelleris Reader Awards
Emirates named Best Long-haul Airline

Skytrax World Airline Awards
Emirates named World's Best Airline

Skytrax World Airline Awards
Emirates awarded for World's Best Inflight Entertainment

Skytrax World Airline Awards
Emirates named Best Middle East Airline

Business Traveller Middle East Awards
Emirates named Best Airline Worldwide

Business Traveller Middle East Awards
Emirates named Airline with the Best Business Class

Business Traveller Middle East Awards
Emirates named Airline with the Best Economy Class

Business Traveller Middle East Awards
Emirates named Best Regional Airline Serving the Middle East

World Travel Awards for the Middle East
Emirates named the Middle East's Leading Airline Business Class

World Travel Awards for the Middle East
Emirates named the Middle East's Leading Airline Rewards Programme

World Travel Awards for the Middle East
Emirates named the Middle East's Leading Airline Website

Sabq Tourism Awards
Emirates named Best Arab Airline 2013

Route network

Africa

Algiers
Casablanca
Tunis
Tripoli
Dakar
Conakry
Abidjan
Accra
Abuja
Lagos
Luanda
Cape Town
Durban
Johannesburg
Harare
Lusaka
Dar Es Salaam
Nairobi
Entebbe
Addis Ababa
Khartoum
Cairo
Seychelles
Mauritius

Asia

Kabul
Sialkot
Peshawar
Islamabad
Lahore
Karachi
Delhi
Ahmedabad
Mumbai
Kolkata
Dhaka
Hyderabad
Bengaluru
Chennai
Kozhikode
Kochi
Thiruvananthapuram
Colombo
Male
Bangkok
Phuket
Kuala Lumpur
Singapore
Jakarta

Ho Chi Minh City
Manilla
Hong Kong
Taipei
Guangzhou
Beijing
Seoul
Osaka
Tokyo

Australasia

Broome
Port Hedland
Karratha
Exmouth
Newman
Paraburdoo
Geraldton
Perth
Kalgoorlie
Uluru (Ayers Rock)
Darwin
Gove
Weipa
Cairns
Townsville
Hamilton Island
Mackay
Moranbah
Rockhampton
Gladstone
Bunderberg
Hervey Bay
Brisbane
Gold Coast
Coffs Harbour
Port Macquarie
Lord Howe Island
Newcastle
Sydney

Canberra
Mount Hotham
Melbourne
Adelaide
Port Lincoln
Mildura
Wagga Wagga
Albury
Dubbo
Tamworth
Armidale
Roma
Biloela
Emerald
Blackall
Charleville
Alice Springs
Longreach
Mount Isa
Cloncurry
Horn Island
Devonport
Launceston
Hobart
Auckland
Wellington
Christchurch
Queenstown

Middle East

Sanaía
Jeddah
Madinah
Amman
Beirut
Riyadh
Dammam
Dubai
Muscat
Doha
Bahrain
Kuwait City
Basra
Damascus
Beirut
Gerbil
Baghdad
Tehran
Kabul

Europe

Glasgow
Dublin
Birmingham
London
Newcastle
Manchester
Oslo
Stockholm
St. Petersburg
Moscow
Copenhagen
Warsaw
Hamburg
Amsterdam
Dusseldorf
Prague
Brussels
Frankfurt
Munich
Paris
Zurich
Vienna

Kiev
Budapest
Venice
Geneva
Lyon
Nice
Milan
Barcelona
Madrid
Lisbon
Rome
Malta
Athens
Istanbul
Larnaca

Americas

Buenos Aires
Sao Paulo
Rio De Janeiro
Seattle
Los Angeles
San Francisco
Chicago
Toronto
Dallas
Houston
Boston
New York
Washington, DC

BOOST YOUR

CANDIDACY

PART 3

Contents
Of this Session

"If you change the way you look at things, the things you look at change"

- *Dr. Wayne Dyer*

APPLICATION
GUIDANCE

Ulterior Motives

It is true to say that job applications are primarily used to collect data for the purpose of evaluating skills, qualifications, employment history and motives, however, what most individuals don't realise is that there is an ulterior motive.

From the airline's perspective, the form serves a number of other important purposes, namely: To evaluate the applicant's literacy, ability to follow instructions, penmanship and communication skills. Recruiters will be looking or any excuse to thin the pack, so a careless applicant, or one who doesn't follow instructions, will quickly disqualify themselves, and the recruiter will not take the time to decipher what is written on it.

Unlike resume's, which are unique to each individual, the standardised format of an application form allows selectors to quickly peruse and compare each form, and it is easy to see which candidates have made an effort and those who haven't.

Consider the following examples.

I CURRENTLY WORK AS A FREELANCE HAIRDRESSER AND HAVE WORKED IN CLIENT FACING ROLES FOR MORE THAN 8 YEARS. I AM LOOKING FOR A CHANGE IN MY LIFE DIRECTION AND FEEL THAT A CAREER AS CABIN CREW WILL GIVE ME THIS.

I curently work as freelance hairdresser & have worked in client facing roles fore more than 8 years. I am looking for a change in my life direction and feel that that a career as cabin crew will give me this.

The first example is tidy and creates a positive impression of the candidate. Meanwhile, the second example is messy, full of typos and barely legible. It is clear that the candidate jumped straight in without planning. Hardly a positive first impression.

To ensure this doesn't happen to your application form, take note of the following guidelines.

Important

GUIDELINES

Before you begin

- Read through the form to familiarise yourself with the questions and any specific instructions
- Gather materials: Black pens, a pencil and eraser
- Gather the necessary information:
    Personal details: Passport, contact information, vital statistics
    Education and training information: Qualifications, dates, results
    Employment History: Names, addresses, key dates
- Plan what you want to write in each section, taking note of the space available

Completing the form

- Set aside sufficient time and minimise distractions
- Re-read the instructions as you work on each section
- Write clearly and neatly: Block capitals are tidy and easy to read
- Keep your text within the space provided (Practice on a blank sheet of paper if you are unsure of the space available)
- Answer every question and use 'Not Applicable' or 'N/A' where questions are not relevant to you
- Keep the tone positive and be mindful not to volunteer negative information
- Be concise and avoid continuations on separate sheets of paper. If unavoidable, remember to clearly state your name and detail which part of the application form it is linked to

Finishing off

- If time permits, walk away for a few hours and return with a fresh pair of eyes
- Finish off with a quick proofread and make any necessary adjustments if there are typos, grammatical errors and inaccuracies
- If time permits, make a copy of the final form for future reference

Mailing off the form

- Select an envelope that is large enough not to require any folding of the form
- Address the envelope correctly and apply the correct postage
- Send it off before the closing date

Stretching

THE TRUTH

If you are thinking about padding out your application form in order to increase your chances of being hired, you wouldn't be the first. Many candidates are tempted to stretch the truth either to gain a favourable advantage or as a means to cover undesirable facts.

Airlines are savvy to this idea and often verify the details you include within it. So, beware that exaggerations and untruths can come back to haunt you if you are quizzed about them at the interview, or later in employment. If you are caught, any future you may have had with the airline will be devastated.

What are the chances of your information being verified? 100%. This is an industry that places high importance on security, and an airline is not going to take any risks with providing airside passes to just anyone. Your references will be contacted and your background checked, so be safe and don't take any unnecessary risks. There are many things you can do to boost your candidacy and minimise imperfections, and it just isn't worth the risk.

Minimise

A FRAGMENTED WORK HISTORY

A fragmented work history will give the impression of a job hopper and will raise serious doubts about your commitment. Whether the assumption is true or not, it surely doesn't present a favourable impression,

Whatever the reason, whether you have held temporary agency contracts, have been struggling to find something that you can feel committed to, or have simply been trying to gain a more rounded skill-set, it is important to draw attention away from it so that you can avoid any negative and rash assumptions being made.

Here are some options:

Eliminate

Where a position holds little or no relevance, was held only briefly, is dated, or was only held part time, you may be able to safely exclude it from your application. Beware that you should only do this if doing so will not create damaging gaps.

Spring into summer

Instead of listing specific dates for summer jobs, you can simply state Summer 20xx to Spring 20xx.

Consecutive combining

Where several similar consecutive jobs appear or were provided by the same agency, you can combine them into one chunk, for example:

2004–2006 Receptionist
Aztec Hotel & Spa, Bloomfields Leisure, Trina's Hair & Beauty Salon

2001–2003 Customer service manager
Multi-national business agency

Fill gaps in employment

If you have gaps in your employment history, you may be asked to elaborate on these. Whatever your reasons: whether it was for maternity leave, study or a travel break, you need to observe caution about revealing too much about your personal circumstances. Revealing that you had taken maternity leave will highlight your parental status and could be used as a tool to discriminate against you.

If you were doing anything during the gaps, paid or unpaid, inserting them in place of the gap will add much needed bulk and minimise the appearance of the gaps.

For example:

Summer 2004–Spring 2005   Travelled around Europe
July 2001–November 2001   Study break

How to deal

WITH BEING

If you have a termination on your record, the recruiters will not care if the termination was unjust, unfair or has a good explanation, a termination is a big red flag, so you need to do everything you can to avoid disclosing it.

In the first instance, you may choose to omit the information. Omitting details is not the same as telling an outright lie or making a false statement. When asked for reference details, simply choose another referee.

If you have just been fired from your most recent employment, they will not know unless you tell them. So you could mark your employment to present and leave it at that. If asked if they can call your employer for a reference, it would not raise any eyebrows if you respectfully decline due to your ongoing employment.

The third option is to take proactive measures to have the termination designation changed.

If the termination occurred some time ago, it is more likely that the employer will be open to changing the designation if you accept responsibility and demonstrate a sincere regret for the situation. Simply advise them that the termination is damaging your chances of gaining employment and you would like the designation changed to something neutral, such as laid off or resigned.

If you would feel uncomfortable or unethical to omit such a detail and would prefer to take accountability for what happened, be sure to downplay the termination on your application form by simply stating 'will explain at interview'. You will have some damage control to contend with, so remember to accept the mistake, don't blame others and don't make any excuses. Stick to the facts, point out what went wrong and what you have learned from the experience.

Whichever route you take, there is a risk. Either you not be hired by admitting to the termination or you may not be hired because you did not disclose it and were caught out. The decision has to be yours.

Communicate

YOUR SUITABILITY

The most important aspect of your application form is that you must communicate your suitability for the position clearly by highlighting the skills and experience that are relevant and transferable. Using a selection of key words that are often used to describe the cabin crew position will achieve this.

For example, a salon receptionist may include the following:

- Delivered the highest level of customer service
- Ensured customer comfort
- Provided a friendly and professional service
- Assisted with enquiries and resolved complaints

These short action statements identify customer service experience and the ability to handle specific responsibilities that are required of cabin crew. It would be clear to any airline that this candidate has the necessary experience and is adequately qualified for the position.

Use

ACTION PHRASES

When describing your duties, three to five action phrases have a better impact than complete sentences or generic job descriptions. Consider the following examples:

Complete sentence
'As a call centre officer, I answer customer queries and complaints over the telephone'

Action statement
'Addressed customer queries and resolved complaints'

The former example has a passive tone and is unnecessarily wordy, whereas the latter example uses an active and punchy tone. Such statements will grab the attention of the reader much more readily than lengthy paragraphs.

Leverage

YOUR LEISURE INTERESTS

Recreational interests create depth and humanises your character. A targeted list, which focuses on relevant skills, will form an immediate and positive impression. Such interests also serve as excellent sources of additional skills and experiences, which can be advantageous if you lack relevant experience in a work environment.

Generalised list statements such as: 'reading, watching television, sport and socialising' should be avoided, as should unprofessional statements such as: 'I enjoy spending time with my mates, hitting the town and going out on the razz".

Take a look at the following example:

"I have been keen on netball for as long as I can remember and am an active member of my local netball club where I have been captain of the team for 3 years. I have an active interest in nature, and regularly get involved with and manage conservation assignments. To relax, I attend yoga and meditation classes, which help to keep me focused and relieve any build-up of stress.'

This statement gives an immediate impression of someone who is balanced and committed. Their interests highlight several admirable qualities such as team spirit and leadership, and it also details their methods of stress management. A recruitment office would form a positive impression of the candidate based on a statement such as this.

Be mindful about over-indulging in your leisure interests, as the recruiter may get the impression that your hobbies will take priority over your work.

The power
OF A PERSONAL STATEMENT

At the end of most application forms, you will be presented with some form of additional information box. This box may simply state 'Additional Information', or it could be more specific, such as: Please state your reason for applying and why you feel you are suited to the position of cabin crew?

Essentially, this is an opportunity to sell yourself and should never remain blank. Use it to provide a power statement that summarises your experience, highlights your key skills, and shares your motives all within a few short paragraphs.

Consider the following example:

'As you will note, I have eight years experience within the retail industry. Within which, I have built extensive customer relations, team working and supervisory experience, which has also greatly enhanced my communication and interpersonal skills.

With these skills and experiences, combined with my passion for the airline industry, my motivation to succeed, strong attention to detail, and unparalleled work ethic, I am confident that I will make a positive contribution to the airline and excel as a member of the Fly High cabin crew team."

The above example is concise. It focuses on what the candidate can offer the airline, rather than what the airline can offer the candidate, and it showcases skills and experiences that are an asset for a cabin crew position.

Highlight career progression

If you have remained with an employer for several years, but have progressed through the ranks, you can make your progression more obvious by listing each position as you would a new job.

List your awards

Outstanding excellence will show commitment and talent, so if you have achieved any awards through your activities, be sure to list them. Make sure the achievements are recent though, as outdated awards may give the impression that you haven't achieved anything since.

Get permission from referees

Always get permission from the person(s) you state as your referee(s) and give them a copy of your application form or resume to help them write a relevant reference that highlights your most important points.

Emirates Airlines

Application for Cabin Crew Employment

All information supplied will be treated as confidential.
Subject to meeting the eligibility criteria, you will be invited to attend our next selection day.
Correct information will be a condition of employment.

Full Name (Mr / Mrs / Ms)   **JANE DOE**   Date Available   **29/01/11**

Present Address	Permanent Address (If different)
22 ANY STREET ANY TOWN ANY WHERE	N/A

Post Code	**AN2 6DG**	Country	**U.K**	Post Code	**N/A**	Country	**N/A**

Please give telephone numbers in the format: Country Code + City/Mobile Code + Phone Number

Telephone (Residence)	44 1179 637264	Telephone (Residence)	N/A
Telephone (Mobile)	44 798 837472	Telephone (Mobile)	N/A
Email	JANE.DOE@ANYMAIL.COM		

Personal Information

Passport Number:	2048374638	Expiry Date:	09/2021
Date of Birth:	11/09/1979	Gender:	FEMALE
Marital Status:	SINGLE	Nationality:	BRITISH

Height (cm)	154	Weight (kg)	49

Do you have tattoos or body piercings?   **NO**   If yes, please specify   **N/A**

How would you rate your ability to swim?   **AVERAGE ABILITY UNAIDED**

Education

Please continue on a separate sheet if necessary

From	To	Name & Address of School/College	Subject(s)	Results
09/99	07/01	ANY COLLEGE - ANY WHERE - AN8 7KD	HAIRDRESSING	NVQ 3 - DISTINCTION
09/98	07/99	ANY COLLEGE - ANY WHERE - AN8 7KD	HAIRDRESSING	NVQ 2 - MERIT
09/97	07/98	ANY COLLEGE - ANY WHERE - AN8 7KD	HAIRDRESSING	NVQ 1 - DISTINCTION
09/91	07/96	ANY SCHOOL - ANY WHERE - AN8 375	ENGLISH / GEOGRAPHY FRENCH / ART / CDT MATHS / SCIENCE / MATHS	8 GCSE'S GRADE A-C

Present/Last Employer

Employer:	SELF EMPLOYED	From:	01/02/03	To:	PRESENT
Position:	HAIRDRESSER	Salary:	15,000 PA	
Address:	N/A	Notice Required:	NONE	
		Reason for Leaving:	TO PURSUE A CAREER AS CABIN CREW	

Responsibilities:
MANAGE AND MAINTAIN A CUSTOMER BASE OF OVER 100 CLIENTS
CONSULT AND ADVISE CUSTOMERS
ENSURE CUSTOMER SATISFACTION
PROVIDE A FRIENDLY AND PROFESSIONAL SERVICE
MAINTAIN UP TO DATE RECORDS AND ACCOUNTS

Previous Employment   Please continue on a separate sheet if necessary

Employer: TRINA'S HAIR SALON   From: 16/02/00   To: 01/02/03
Address: 159 ANY CITY CENTRE ANY TOWN - AN9 6DJ
Responsibilities: SUPERVISED AND TRAINED A TEAM OF FOUR JUNIOR-LEVEL STYLISTS - HIRED WORK EXPERIENCE STUDENTS - CONSULTED AND ADVISED CUSTOMERS - ENSURED CUSTOMER COMFORT AND SATISFACTION - PROVIDED A FRIENDLY AND PROFESSIONAL SERVICE
Position: SENIOR HAIR STYLIST
Reason for Leaving: TO PURSUE FREELANCE OPPORTUNITY

Employer: TRINA'S HAIR SALON   From: 05/04/98   To: 16/08/00
Address: 159 ANY CITY CENTRE ANY TOWN - AN9 6DJ
Responsibilities: CONSULTED AND ADVISED CUSTOMERS - ENSURED CUSTOMER COMFORT AND SATISFACTION - PROVIDED A FRIENDLY AND PROFESSIONAL SERVICE
Position: JUNIOR HAIR STYLIST
Reason for Leaving: TO PURSUE PROMOTION OPPORTUNITY

Employer: MACEY'S HAIR SALON   From: 24/07/97   To: 05/04/98
Address: 378 ANY CITY CENTRE ANY TOWN - AN5 6SJ
Responsibilities: DELIVERED THE HIGHEST LEVEL OF CUSTOMER SERVICE - ENSURED CUSTOMER COMFORT - PROVIDED A FRIENDLY AND PROFESSIONAL SERVICE - ASSISTED WITH ENQUIRIES AND RESOLVED COMPLAINTS
Position: RECEPTIONIST
Reason for Leaving: TO PURSUE PROMOTION OPPORTUNITY

Please explain any gaps in unemployment
UPON LEAVING SCHOOL IN 1996, I SPENT A YEAR TRAVELLING BEFORE MOVING INTO EMPLOYMENT

Please list any voluntary work
FOR THE LAST THREE YEARS, I HAVE VOLUNTEERED AT THE SAMARITANS HOMELESS SHELTER DURING THE CHRISTMAS PERIOD, WHERE I HELP COOK AND SERVE BEVERAGES

Additional Training

Give details of any first aid and/or nursing qualifications

BRITISH RED CROSS - BASIC FIRST AID TRAINING - 09/2006

Give details of languages spoken and abilities

ENGLISH - NATIVE LANGUAGE
FRENCH - READ, WRITE AND SPEAK FLUENTLY
SPANISH - BASIC CONVERSATIONAL ABILITY

Give details of any other training

I HAVE ATTENDED, AND PASSED, SHORT COURSES IN LEADERSHIP AND COMMUNICATION

Hobbies/Outside Interests

I HAVE BEEN KEEN ON NETBALL FOR AS LONG AS I CAN REMEMBER AND AM AN ACTIVE MEMBER OF MY LOCAL NETBALL CLUB WHERE I HAVE BEEN CAPTAIN OF THE TEAM FOR 3 YEARS. I HAVE AN ACTIVE INTEREST IN NATURE, AND REGULARLY GET INVOLVED WITH AND MANAGE CONSERVATION ASSIGNMENTS. TO RELAX, I ATTEND YOGA AND MEDITATION CLASSES, WHICH HELP TO KEEP ME FOCUSED AND RELIEVE ANY BUILD-UP OF STRESS

Use the following space to provide any further information that you feel will benefit your application

AS YOU WILL NOTE, I HAVE EIGHT YEARS EXPERIENCE WITHIN THE RETAIL INDUSTRY, WITHIN WHICH, I HAVE BUILT EXTENSIVE CUSTOMER RELATIONS, TEAM WORKING AND SUPERVISORY EXPERIENCE, WHICH HAS ALSO GREATLY ENHANCED MY COMMUNICATION AND INTERPERSONAL SKILLS.

WITH THESE SKILLS AND EXPERIENCES, COMBINED WITH MY PASSION FOR THE AIRLINE INDUSTRY, MY MOTIVATION TO SUCCEED, STRONG ATTENTION TO DETAIL, AND UNPARALLELED WORK ETHIC, I AM CONFIDENT THAT I WILL MAKE A POSITIVE CONTRIBUTION TO THE AIRLINE AND EXCEL AS A MEMBER OF THE FLY HIGH CABIN CREW TEAM.

Declaration

Have you ever been convicted of a criminal offence which, at the date of application, is not a spent conviction as defined in the Rehabilitation of Offenders Act 1974?   Yes/No
If yes, then such convictions must be disclosed below.

N/A

Have you ever been refused entry, or deported from a foreign country?   Yes/No
If yes, please provide further details.

N/A

The details provided on this application are correct to my knowledge and belief. I understand that my application may be rejected or that I may be dismissed for withholding relevant information or giving false information. I am aware that my employment with Emirates will be subject to satisfactory references, medical form and criminal record checks.

Signature   Date   05/01/2011

RESUME

GUIDANCE

Influence

THE DIRECTION OF THE INTERVIEW

Because the recruiters will have no information about you beyond this document, it will be a major influence in the nature and direction of the interview. This allows an element of predictability and makes it a very powerful document indeed.

With such a valuable tool at your disposal, it is important that it represents the best you have to offer. If your resume is strong, it will focus the recruiter's questioning on information that presents your image strongly. The following guidelines will help you achieve this.

Appearance

Colour

Use colour sparingly. Black text, with a consistent injection of colour for the headings will make your resume more pleasing to the human eye. Colour paper should be avoided as scanning or photocopying will be problematic.

Length

For this type of position, one or two pages is ideal. However, don't be constrained by this advice if doing so will mean that you have to squeeze your data in and use a tiny 8 point font, If you do find your resume going beyond this quota, be sure that it isn't being filled with unnecessary, unfocused or excessive detail.

Single or double sided?

Double sided prints are harder to photocopy and risk show through. Stick to single sided prints for a cleaner look.

Staples

Never staple your sheets together. Staples are inconvenient for the employer if they need to photocopy or scan your resume, plus the reviewer may want to view the pages side by side. A traditional paper clip is acceptable.

Identification

Be sure all of the pages include your name and page numbers so they can be easily reconnected should they become separated.

Action
VERBS

Action verbs express action. They are positive, powerful and directive, and should be used abundantly throughout your résumé.

Notice how using direct action verbs make the sentence powerful:

"As a hairdresser, I <u>consulted</u> with clients and <u>provided</u> advice"

The following page contains an extensive list of action verbs. Use them abundently throughout your resume and application form.

Action verbs

Achieved
Addressed
Advocated
Allocated
Analysed
Anticipated
Appraised
Approved
Arbitrated
Arranged
Assembled
Assessed
Attained
Authored
Balanced
Budgeted
Built
Calculated
Catalogued
Clarified
Classified
Coached
Collaborated
Collected
Communicated
Compiled
Conceptualised
Consolidated
Consulted
Contracted
Conveyed
Convinced
Coordinated

Corresponded
Counselled
Created
Critiqued
Customised
Delegated
Demonstrated
Designed
Developed
Directed
Enlisted
Established
Evaluated
Examined
Executed
Expedited
Explained
Expressed
Fabricated
Facilitated
Forecasted
Formulated
Founded
Generated
Guided
Handled
Identified
Illustrated
Implemented
Improved
Incorporated
Increased
Influenced

Informed
Initiated
Inspected
Instituted
Integrated
Interpreted
Interviewed
Introduced
Invented
Investigated
Lectured
Led
Listened
Litigated
Maintained
Marketed
Mediated
Moderated
Motivated
Negotiated
Operated
Organised
Originated
Overhauled
Oversaw
Participated
Performed
Persuaded
Pioneered
Planned
Presented
Produced
Projected

Promoted
Publicised
Recommended
Recruited
Reduced
Referred
Repaired
Reported
Represented
Researched
Resolved
Review
Reviewed
Revitalised
Scheduled
Shaped
Solved
Spearheaded
Spoke
Strengthened
Suggested
Summarised
Supervised
Systematised
Taught
Trained
Translated
Upgrades
Wrote

Format

There are three basic resume formats:

Chronological:

The chronological resume highlights the dates, places of employment and job titles, and is most effective for candidates who have a strong, solid work history. It is less effective for those who want to disguise gaps in employment or frequent job changes.

Functional:

A functional resume focuses on skills and experience, rather than work history. Its ability to accentuate your transferable skills and detract attention from your career history makes it better suited to those who want to downplay an extreme career change or a chequered employment history. This style is less useful if you have limited work experience, as there will be little to highlight.

Combination:

The combination resume, as the name implies, is a combination of the chronological and functional formats. It highlights both your work history and your transferable skills, and is most effective when you have a great deal of transferable skills and a solid work history.

Outline

For the purpose of a cabin crew position, I have listed possible resume sections below, in their suggested order:

Applicant information

At the beginning of the résumé, include your name, your home mailing address, your telephone number(s), and your e-mail address. If you have both temporary and permanent addresses, include them both.

Objective statement (Optional)

An objective is a short statement, which defines your career goals. It gives your resume focus and shows that you have given consideration to your career direction.

Examples:

Seeking to utilise extensive customer service experience and exceptional communicative ability within a cabin crew role.

Seeking to pursue a cabin crew position with an airline that rewards commitment and hard work, and offers opportunities to progress.

Tip: If you include an objective, focus your attention on what you can do for the employer, not what the employer can do for you.

Key skills (Optional)

The key skills section provides a fantastic opportunity for you to quickly express your suitability for the role and show what transferable skills your will bring to the position. Additionally, it will bulk out your resume with the keywords needed for OCR scanning technology.

Key skills to consider are:

- Communication Skills
- Interpersonal Ability
- Customer Focus
- Team Player
- Problem Solver
- Leadership

Employment history

Your employment history should be displayed in reverse chronological order (that is starting with your most recent position and working backwards). This should include: the name of the organisation, the position held, the period of employment, the duties performed and results achieved.

The period of employment should include both the start and end dates, and can consist of only the month and year.

When describing your duties use action phrases, rather than compete sentences or generic job descriptions, and list any accomplishments that back up any key skill statements that you have made. For example, if you have stated 'extensive leadership experience' you can use a short action statement such as: "Supervised and trained a team of four junior-level stylists".

If some entries are more relevant to the cabin crew position, emphasise these and provide only summaries for those of less significance..

Other relevant experience (Optional)

Employment history is a broad term that can include relevant internships, summer or seasonal jobs, part time work, and voluntary placements. This is especially important if you have little paid experience.

Education summary

Starting with the most recent and working backwards, include the schools/colleges/universities you have attended. Within each entry, include the year of completion ("In progress" or "expected" are acceptable, if necessary) and award(s) you achieved.

Certifications (Optional)

If you have attended any formal certification courses, e.g., First aid, life saving, then list the details here noting the institution name, date and certification awarded.

Activities & Interests (Optional)

Recreational interests reveal a great deal about your personality and create depth to your character. They also serve as excellent sources of additional skills and experiences, which can be advantageous if you lack certain skills and/or experience.

Generalised list statements such as: 'reading, watching television, sport and socialising' should be avoided, as should unprofessional statements such as: 'I enjoy spending time with my mates, hitting the town and going out on the razz".

Here is an example: 'I have been keen on netball for as long as I can remember and am an active member of my local netball club where I have been captain of the team for 3 years. I have an active interest in nature, and regularly get involved with and manage conservation assignments. To relax, I attend yoga and meditation classes, which help to keep me focused and relieve any build-up of stress.'

This statement gives an immediate impression of someone who is balanced and committed. Their interests highlight several admirable qualities such as team spirit and leadership, and it also details their methods of stress management. A recruitment office would form a positive impression of the candidate based on a statement such as this.

Be mindful about over-indulging in your leisure interests, as the recruiter may get the impression that your hobbies will take priority over your work.

Languages (Optional)

If you have more than one language ability, indicate whether you speak, read, and/or write the language, and include the level to which you are proficient, such as: native, fluent, proficient or basic conversational ability.

References (Optional)

Unless specifically requested, the inclusion of reference information is completely optional.

When listing your references, be sure to include: Name, title, professional relationship to you (e.g. Supervisor, manager and team leader) telephone number and mailing address.

If you decide not to include details, a simple statement such as "References are available on request" is sufficient.

Jane Doe

Seeking to pursue a cabin crew position with an airline that rewards commitment and hard work, and offers opportunities to progress.

16 Any Road • Any Where
Any Town • AN8 9SE
United Kingdom

+44 (0)4587 875848
Jane.Doe@Anymail.com

Key Skills

Communication Skills
Exhibits exceptional written and verbal communication skills, and is adept at communicating effectively with people at all levels, and in a manner appropriate to the audience.

Interpersonal Ability
Unsurpassed interpersonal skills with a proven ability to quickly develop and maintain relationships with customers and colleagues.

Customer Focus
Experienced at providing a high quality service to customers at all levels, and skilled at effectively dealing with and resolving complaints.

Team Spirited
Skilled team player who adapts quickly to different team dynamics and excels at building trusting relationships with colleagues at all levels.

Employment History

Freelance Hairdresser   Feb '03 - Present
- » Manage and maintain a customer base of over 100 clients
- » Consult and advise customers
- » Ensure customer satisfaction
- » Provide a friendly and professional service
- » Maintain up to date records and accounts

Trina's Hair Salon | Senior Stylist   Aug '00 – Feb '03
- » Supervised and trained a team of four junior-level stylists
- » Hired work experience students
- » Consulted and advised customers
- » Ensured customer comfort and satisfaction
- » Provided a friendly and professional service

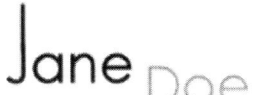

Jane Doe

Continued from page 1...

My confident and friendly nature will enable me to fit in and complement your existing team

Employment History

Trina's Hair Salon - Junior Stylist	April '98 – Aug '00

» Consulted and advised customers

» Ensured customer comfort and satisfaction

» Provided a friendly and professional service

Macey's Hair Salon - Receptionist	July '96 – April '98

» Delivered the highest level of customer service

» Ensured customer comfort

» Provided a friendly and professional service

» Assisted with enquiries and resolved complaints

Education Summary

Any College (2001)	NVQ 3 - Hairdressing
Any College (1999)	NVQ 2 - Hairdressing
Any College (1998)	NVQ 1 – Hairdressing
Any High School (1996)	11 GCSE's (grade A–D)

Certifications

British Red Cross	Basic First Aid – Sept '06

Languages

Fluent in spoken and written Spanish
Basic conversational ability in French

Activities & Interests

I have been keen on netball for as long as I can remember and am an active member of my local netball club where I have been captain of the team for 3 years. I have an active interest in nature, and regularly get involved with and manage conservation assignments. To relax, I attend yoga and meditation classes, which help to keep me focused and relieve any build-up of stress

16 Any Road • Any Where
Any Town • AN8 9SE
United Kingdom

+44 (0)4587 875848
Jane.Doe@Anymail.com

"You have brains in your head. You have feet in your shoes. You can steer yourself in any direction you CHOOSE!

- *Dr. Seuss*

PRODUCE POLISHED
PHOTOGRAPHS

Strict

STANDARDS

The requisition of photographs is so much more than a simple vanity requirement, and I cannot emphasise their importance enough. Not only will they serve as a visual reminder for the recruiters to refer back to throughout the assessment process, but they are also used to make hiring decisions long after the interview is over. Emirates place a great deal of value on the photographs, and have very strict requirements about their presentation. For this reason, it is important that you use the following guidelines to create the very best lasting impression.

Requirements

A head and shoulder shot, generally in the form of a 45 x 35 mm passport photograph, and a full-length shot will be required.

Both are subject to specific requirements and it is vital that you observe those to the letter. I am not kidding. Emirates will not accept your application if the photos do not meet the requirements stated.

Formal Attire

Business attire is the minimum acceptable standard for Emirates.

As with your interview day attire, be sure to select an outfit which is good quality and tailored. You can pin the back in if needed, but be sure the suit is a suitable length and style.

A solid backdrop

Emirates requrie a solid backdrop for a clean and uncluttered appearance. Do not under any circumstances use a bed sheet for the backdrop, and avoid digitally Photoshopped images as your photos will be rejected. Professionally produced photos are the way to go.

Polish your appearance

Photographs tend to exaggerate complexion issues and flatten your features, so use cosmetics to enhance your cheeks, lips and eyes, and apply concealer to diminish spots and blemishes. This goes for gents too.

Contouring and highlight is a technique that can be used to create depth, balance your face shape, play down flaws, and emphasise assets. Contouring uses a dark shade and is used to recede areas, while highlighting uses a light shade and is used to protrude areas.

Try it out and see what a difference it makes to your look.

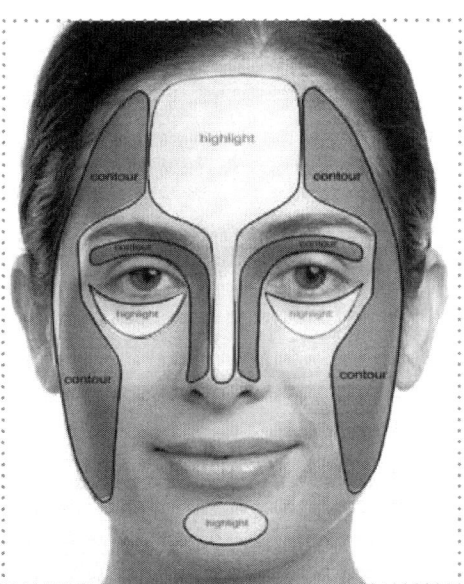

If you suffer from redness, the camera will pick it up and emphasise it further, so apply some green corrective concealer underneath your foundation to conceal it. Use these with caution as they are very heavy duty and can make you look very pale if over applied. Also steer clear of concealers containing spf as these will appear white and garish in photos.

It is important to control the shine, particularly around the t-zone area, as it will reflect strongly in photos. For minor shine issues, a powder foundation should do the trick. For more problematic skin, an oil absorbing moisturiser or oil balancing gel may be more suitable.

Use eye drops to make your eyes glisten and clear any redness. And for wide awake eyes, try directing your gaze slightly above the camera.

Be sure your hair is neat and well groomed, as frizzy hair or loose ends can be exaggerated in pictures.

For an instant chin tuck, have the photographer position the camera at or just above eye level for the most flattering facial shot.

Summon a warm smile

A warm and sincere smile will complete the look, but creating a beautiful smile on demand is a learned skill, which needs to be practiced.

The fake smile, aptly named the 'Pan-Am Smile' because of the flight attendants of Pan-American Airlines, is simply a courtesy smile that will not translate well in your photos. A 'Duchenne Smile', on the other hand, will provide the most beautiful and sincere looking smile, and this is the smile we are looking to achieve.

Here are some tips that will assist you in generating your photo perfect smile.

Produce a natural smile

The most beautiful smiles are the ones that are natural. If you are using a professional photographer, they will be skilled at drawing out your natural smile, but if you are using an unskilled family member, you will need to channel some of your inner happiness. This can be achieved by thinking of a genuine reason to smile, such as recalling a happy memory, looking at a silly picture, or remembering a good joke.

Fake it till you make it

When it is simply impossible to summons a genuine smile, you will need to fake it. Here are some guidelines that will help.

Time it right:

The secret to producing a relaxed and natural smile is to time it so that you don't have to hold it for too long. Try looking away from the camera, then just before the photograph is taken, face the camera and smile.

Use your eyes:

Smiling eyes are required to complete the look. To achieve this effect, imagine the camera is someone you really fancy. Raise your eyebrows and cheekbones a little, and slightly squint the corners of your eyes. Notice the amazing transformation this creates.

Pan-Am Smile

Duchenne Smile

Copyright Paul Ekman 2003,
"Emotions Revealed," Owl Books, 2007

POWER UP YOUR
PORTFOLIO

Power up
YOUR PORTFOLIO

Boost your experience

Experience within a customer-facing role is vital, so if this aspect of your application is shallow or weak, you should certainly consider taking on some additional short-term volunteer or evening work to compensate and strengthen your candidacy. Taking on additional work will show initiative and demonstrate a willingness to work and improve.

Take on volunteer work

Volunteering is beneficial to your application in so many ways. Firstly, it will demonstrate a compassionate and caring side to your personality. Secondly, it will enable you to gain experience and flesh out your skill-set. And third, it will show that you are not motivated by monetary gain.

As a side benefit, you will also gain additional referees who can vouch for you.

Learn new skills

Taking the time to learn new skills will demonstrate your continued dedication to self-improvement and your effort in readying yourself for the position. So consider signing up for mini courses that will be relevant to the position, such as first aid, languages, assertiveness, communication, and leadership. Neither will take much time or money, but the value added to your resume will be substantial.

Engage in extra-curricular activities

Extra-curricular activities can be a hidden gem when it comes to learning new skills and are often under-utilised. If you participate in team sports, it can demonstrate your ability to be a team player. If you coach little league, it will demonstrate your ability to be a leader and if you regularly participate in aerobic activities, it will show that you take pride in your health and fitness. So go out there and have some fun while boosting your candidacy all at the same time.

Mind the gaps

If you are between work when you apply, this can create a damaging gap that will need some explaining or give the wrong impression about your motives. Rather than do nothing during this period of downtime, be proactive by taking on some volunteer work, learning a new skill or sign up for a short course at your local college.

GROUP INTERVIEW

PART 4

Contents
Of this Session

"Success is getting what you want. Happiness is wanting what you get"

- Dale Carnegie

HIDDEN
MEANINGS
BEHIND THE GROUP TASKS

What recruiters

ARE REALLY LOOKING FOR

This is the one question I am asked, time and time again. So many candidates overanalyse the process, but the answer is actually very simple. So simple in fact that most of you you will already know what I am going to say.

The recruiters are assessing six key competencies. These are:

- Communication skills
- Interpersonal ability
- Customer focus
- Team spirit
- Leadership
- Initiative

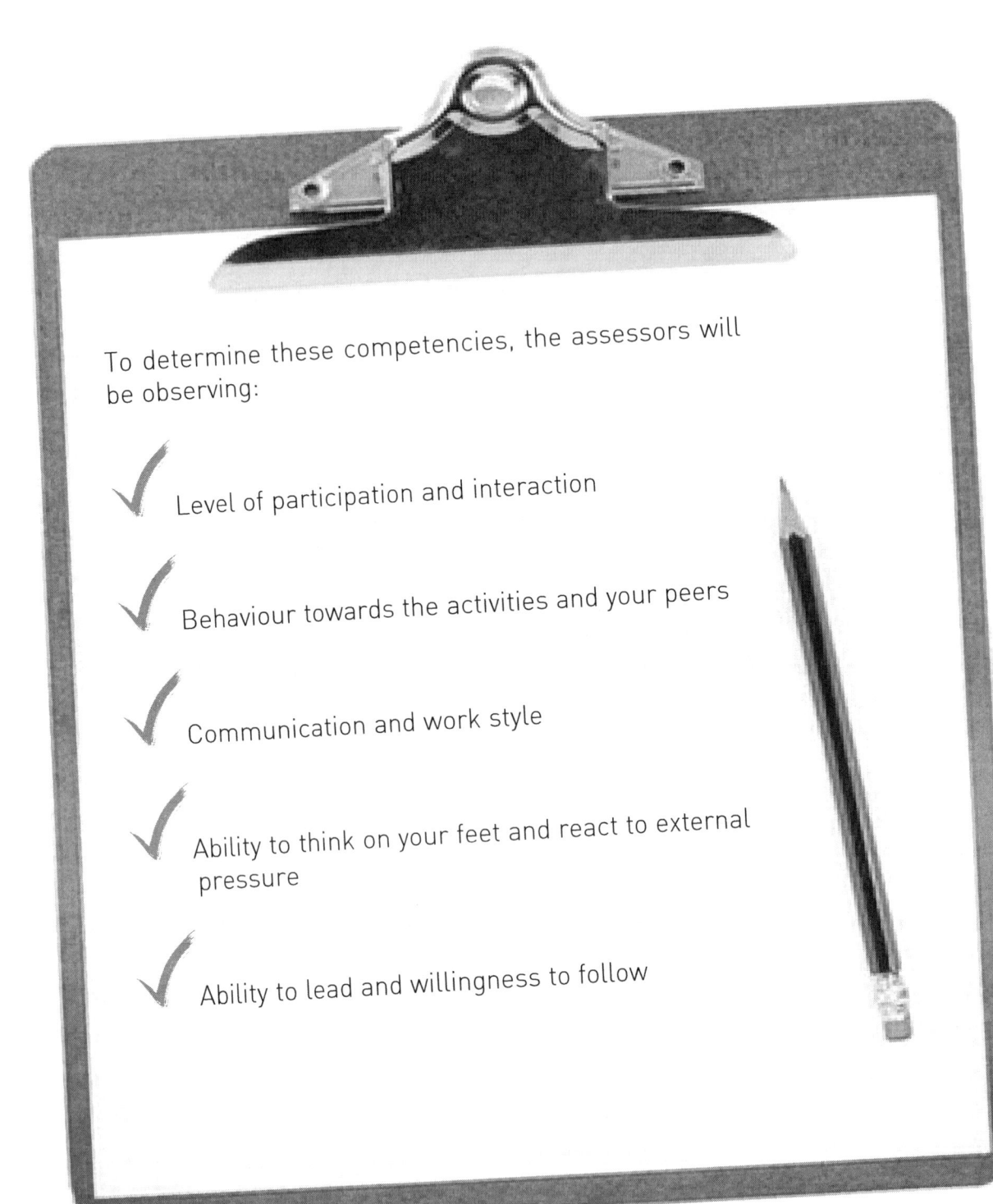

To determine these competencies, the assessors will be observing:

✓ Level of participation and interaction

✓ Behaviour towards the activities and your peers

✓ Communication and work style

✓ Ability to think on your feet and react to external pressure

✓ Ability to lead and willingness to follow

Where confusion

OFTEN OCCURS

Group tasks are designed so that assessors can view and assess these core competencies first hand, and how you behave during each task will be taken as a clear indication of how you may perform in reality. While it goes without saying that how you behave during an interview is not going to be an accurate representation when compared with a real life scenario, it is through your involvement and behaviour, that assessors can identify positive and negative attributes first hand and be able to make better elimination decisions.

Where most individuals often become confused is between the relevancy of the task and what is actually being observed. Because some of the tasks bear no obvious relevance to the cabin crew role, it is easy to overlook the underlying motives and get caught up in the practicalities of the task instead. And herein lies the trick: The outcome of the task itself is irrelevant.

Focusing

ON THE **WRONG!** ELEMENT

During this segment, most candidates are so intently focused on completing the task correctly and on time that they forget to think about their performance. In most cases, the outcome of the task is actually irrelevant. Assessors are more concerned with how well you perform under pressure and in a team environment, how you communicate your ideas, how you interact with others and what role you assume.

When you think back to the group tasks you have participated in, do you notice that they appear to have no right or wrong answer?

As an example, consider the following group topic:

Topic:

The plane has gone down over the Atlantic Ocean. There are eight survivors, but the one surviving life raft only has a capacity for four people. As a **team**, identify four survivors from the following list who you would save and state your reasons why. Select a spokes-person to **present** your decision and explain why you came up with the answer.

You (the flight attendant)   The pope
An ex army general   A surgeon
A pregnant lady   A child
An word class athlete   A nurse

Clearly there is no right answer to this topic, as you wouldn't want to decide such a fate for four people. So what is the point of this task? Take another look at the topic and notice the words I have emphasised are 'team' and 'present'. These are the keys to this task. Assessors are looking to observe how you interact as part of a team, and whether you demonstrate initiative and leadership by volunteering to present the information back to the rest of the group. Most candidates will focus on everything except for those two key points.

Let's take a look at another example: Singing.

Many candidates understand the concept of a discussion or role-play scenario, but just do not understand how singing bears any relevance. Again, this is very simple to comprehend if you read between the lines.

Task:

Many passengers ignore safety demonstrations because they feel they have heard it all before. In an effort to increase safety, Emirates is considering an overhaul of its safety procedures. As a **team**, come up with a new safety demonstration, which will encourage passengers to pay attention to these important briefings.

The demonstration can include appropriate humour, and must be sung according to the melody given to you on the back of the card. The outcome should be no more than **five minutes** in length and **each individual must participate**.

STAND OUT

AS AN INDIVIDUAL

Seven
HEAVENLY VIRTUES

 ## Have fun

However silly or irrelevant the tasks may seem, your active involvement is essential. So, rather than concern yourself about external details, just relax and allow yourself to enjoy the process. This positive viewpoint will reflect well on your character, demonstrate enthusiasm, and make the experience a fun filled one for you.

 ## Contribute

Contributing ideas and making suggestions is another great way to demonstrate your enthusiasm and team spirit. It will show that you are able to express yourself and are keen to get involved.

 ## Volunteer

There are times when no candidate wants to put their neck on the line, so volunteering is a great way to demonstrate your enthusiasm and it will show that you are not afraid to take the initiative.

4 Summarise

Summarising the main points of a discussion is a great way to move past awkward moments of silence and sticking points. The breathing room summarising creates will typically stimulate further ideas and encourage participation. Not only will your peers be grateful for the momentary relief, your communication and leadership ability will also be highlighted.

5 Use names

Remembering people's names will demonstrate your ability to listen and pay attention to detail. Moreover, it will demonstrate a tremendous amount of respect for others and create a lasting impact.

6 Be positive

When you choose to exhibit a positive spirit, people will naturally be drawn towards your character. So, be enthusiastic about the exercises you are asked to undertake and be encouraging towards others.

7 Encourage

If any members of your team remain reserved, encourage their involvement by asking if they have an idea, suggestion or opinion. This shows empathy, consideration and team spirit.

Seven

DEADLY SINS

 ## Over involvement

Getting involved and showing enthusiasm in a task is fantastic, but over involvement and incessant talking can leave others struggling to get involved and may transfer across to assessors as arrogance. Always provide others with an opportunity to provide their opinion.

 ## Under involvement

For assessors to make an informed assessment, active involvement from each individual is essential. Those who are unable to get involved, for whatever reason, will surely be eliminated.

 ## Disputing

Conflicting views are natural, however, a group assessment is neither the time or place to engage in a hostile dispute with other candidates.

4 Criticising

Even if your intentions are honourable and the feedback is constructive, criticising another candidates opinions, actions and ideas may be perceived as an attack. An assessment day is neither the time nor the place.

5 Being negative

Making negative remarks or exhibiting frustration over tasks, peers or previous employers , no matter how harmless it may seem, will raise serious concerns about your attitude and ethics.

6 Being bossy

There is nothing wrong with striving for excellence, however, being dominant and imposing your ideas on others is overbearing and intimidating. This always leads others to feel incompetent.

7 Neglecting to listen

Neglecting to listen to instructions leads to misinterpretations and displays a general lack of enthusiasm. Not listening or talking over others is ignorant and disrespectful.

Active involvement
IS ESSENTIAL . . .

I know it goes without saying, and I've covered this briefly above, but it bears repeating that it is only through your active involvement that recruiters are able to assess your suitability and identify your positive attributes. So however silly or irrelevant the tasks may seem, or how difficult it is to get your opinion across, your involvement is essential.

Rather than concern yourself about external details, just relax and allow yourself to enjoy the process. This positive viewpoint will reflect well on your character, demonstrate enthusiasm, and make the experience a fun filled one for you.

I understand that it can be difficult to get involved when you are in a group of individuals who have big personalities. They set off on a tangent, leaving you feeling like you are on the outside struggling to get in. While these conditions do pose a difficult challenge, it is absolutely essential that you do what you can to be included. Raise your hand if you need to, but whatever you do, don't remain on the outside.

If you suffer from nervousness, understand that it is okay to be nervous, even permissible, but allowing your nerves to keep you from getting involved is not. It is better to risk displaying your nerves than it is to remain silent. At least the recruiters will appreciate your effort. If your nerves are strong to the point that you become debilitated, turn back to part 3 for in-depth guidance, tips and tricks.

. . . But

DON'T OVERDO IT

Getting involved and showing enthusiasm in a task is fantastic, but over involvement and incessant talking can leave others struggling to get involved. This often has the undesirable effect of transferring across to assessors as arrogance. It is important to be balanced.

Have you ever noticed how it is usually the quieter members of the group who seem to be successful, while the confident and active members are often left confused at their elimination?

If you do notice that other members of your team remain reserved or appear to be struggling to get involved, encourage their involvement by asking if they have an idea, suggestion or opinion. This is a clear indication of empathy, consideration and team spirit, and it is these qualities that recruiters will be impressed by.

Your scorecard

To make an effective evaluation, the recruiters will typically refer to a competency rating scale. This scale works on a points based system and the final result will reflect a candidate's suitability for the position.

	-1 Unacceptable	0 Needs Improvement	1 Effective	2 Proficient	3 Outstanding

3	Works effectively as a team member and builds strong relationships within it
0	Remains calm and confident, and responds logically and decisively in difficult situations
3	Understands other people's views and takes them into account
2	Contributes ideas and collaborates with the team
0	Takes a systematic approach to problem solving
3	Speaks with authority and confidence
3	Is thoughtful and tactful when dealing with people
-1	Is conscientious of completing tasks on time
3	Actively supports and encourages others
-1	Participates as an active and contributing member of the team

UNDERCOVER
OPERATIONS

Undercover

OPERATIONS

It is by no means a secret that candidates rarely show their true selves during a formal interview process. They will do their best to say all the right things, hide undesirable traits and say what they think the recruiters want to hear. After all, it is only natural that you'll want to be seen in the best possible light. The problem is, this makes it extremely difficult for personnel to accurately gage whether any one particular candidate is truly a good fit for the job, the airline and its corporate culture, or is just playing a very good part for the interview.

The task of filtering through hundreds or thousands of applicants is an arduous one and, to make matters worse, there are only a few short hours in which to accomplish it.

To relieve some of this pressure, undercover personnel are often placed among the group during recruitment days. It is these undercover officers who pose the greatest threat to your ultimate success, as their primary objective is to filter and eliminate candidates as quickly as possible, and for any reason they see fit. They are largely accountable for the high percentage of failure rates and are the reason why many candidates leave the interview feeling confused about their elimination.

Hidden

ASSESSMENTS

From the moment you step foot on the airline's territory, these officers are watching and judging your every move.

Your personal conduct, how you interact socially and professionally, and the information you reveal. are constantly being scrutinised and assessed. Any mishap or red flags raised during this crucial encounter can land your resume in the rejection pile and you to the nearest exit. There are no second chances.

Within the guise of a fellow candidate, these officers can observe individuals in their relaxed and natural state, and be in a better position to extract information. Unsuspecting candidates openly volunteer information that would never otherwise be revealed, as they are lulled into a false sense of security with seemingly harmless dialogue only to be enticed into mindless gossip and other undesirable behaviours.

During this critical period, officers are observing the reactions of candidates closely as they are encouraged to reciprocate and reveal all sorts of personal and private information. The observations made are then periodically fed back to the recruitment team, who are able to use the information to make informed decisions and better elimination choices in record speed.

It's not

WHAT YOU THINK

These officers are not interested in your level of education, previous successes, or best attributes; they are there to uncover information that could potentially cause problems or inconvenience for Emirates. As such, the information gathered at this level is not necessarily sized up against the Emirates' corporate culture and assessment criteria, but rather the hidden criterion and person specification.

It is the information candidates reveal about their health, age, their likes and dislikes, and sensitive information about their background and personal life that are of interest to these officers. Likewise, they will be very interested to learn how you react to certain kinds of behaviours, people and pressures.

Needless to say, a candidate who displays undesirable behaviour or reveal questionable information will not proceed very far.

Shocking
REVELATIONS

It never seizes to amaze me how much information unsuspecting candidates will reveal when they think they are not being assessed. In many instances, it isn't even necessary to cajole candidates into confessing information, as many will openly share all sorts of things. Is it really any wonder airlines use undercover personnel?

Here are just some of the revelations I have encountered during my on site excursions.

 ## Under the influence

"I'm so nervous I think I must have drunk a whole bottle of wine before I arrived."

 ## Bunking off work

"I had to take a sickie at work just to attend this interview, so it better be worth it."

 ## Admissions of deceit

"I had to lie on my application just to get invited to this interview"

Malicious Backbiting

"Did you see what that girl is wearing? What was she thinking?"
"That girl obviously has no brains. I bet she can't even read."

Negative intentions

"This is such a joke, I wanted to work for . . . but keep failing the damn interview so I have no choice but to apply for this one."
"I just want to work my way into first class so I can meet a rich, good looking guy"

The hangover

"I'm so hung over from last nights bash, I just want to go to sleep. Wake me when it's over."

Slandering the boss

"My stupid boss fired me, so I need this job desperately"

Many of these cases are rather extreme, I admit, however, they are by no means rare - I'm sure you've heard similar comments yourself.

As anyone can appreciate, it is these very mindless and irresponsible comments that undercover officers are seeking.

Innocent
CASUALTIES

Unfortunately, candidates don't need to be malicious or brash to be excluded from the process. A candidate who innocently mentions their looming personal challenges, such as going through a separation, in a custody battle, recently been made redundant, experiencing financial difficulties, or dealing with a close family member who is in poor health, could raise red flags as to their focus and stability. While such challenges are common and entirely understandable, such circumstances are simply deemed too risky for Emirates

What to expect?

While the above shock statements were made by actual caniddates, is it possible that such revelations could also be made by the undercover officers themselves as part of their mini assessment? Absolutely. It is precisely this kind of revelation that officers will use to entice a reaction or a reciprocal response. Be mindful, however, because such assessments aren't always this obvious or extreme. Assessments can be covert and very sneaky, so you always need to be on your guard.

Just as new cabin crew hires are put through an intensive training program, so too are undercover officers. These officers are trained in behavioural analysis and psychological profiling and, with this training, they are able to take on a variety of different roles and employ many different tactics. This makes them very effective at blending in and there is little chance that you will ever be able to identify them with any certainty.

The good news is that simply being aware of their presence and being prepared with a strategy will give you an advantage like no other. In fact, your informed knowledge and inability to be culled by their tricks and traps will make you stand out as a top candidate among the crowd.

Even better still, there is much more that you can do, not only to evade their traps, but also turn them into your greatest ally. All that is required is a conscientious and diligent approach.

Your greatest ally

While it is accurate to say that the purpose of these undercover officers is to expose unsuitable candidates, they also have the power to approve candidates they deem to be exceptional.

If you are able to evade the tricks and traps laid out during this critical process and maintain a friendly, confident, and positive dialogue there will be no reason to pursue you further with trick questions. They will simply move on to another candidate when they are able to remove themselves from your presence. And if you are able to go one step further and create a connection with the officer, not only will you be put forward as a recommendation, but they will actually try to help you to succeed.

So how do you go about impressing these officers?

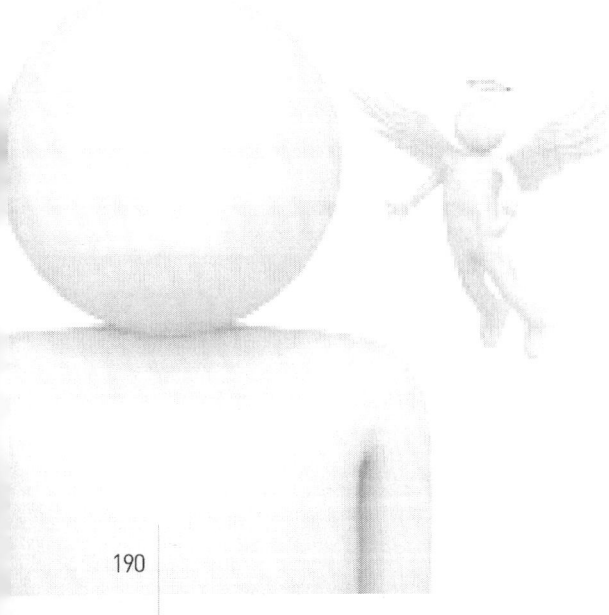

Create

THE RIGHT IMPRESSION

To impress undercover officers, you simply need to treat everyone you meet in the same positive manner. If you are friendly, respectful and supportive towards your fellow candidates, have a positive outlook and are able to demonstrate an enthusiastic attitude towards any activities that you are asked to undertake, the officers will naturally pick up on your positive energy.

Moreover, it is important to remember that anything you say, even in jest or small talk, can and will be used against you. Thus you should avoid volunteering inappropriate information, and your personal life should remain personal.

Naturally this can be easier said than done, so I have devised a line-up of potential scenarios to help you recognise and diffuse any situation you may encounter.

The Lineup

Undercover officers are like actors. They come in many shapes and sizes and their pseudo personalities are just as diverse. Because you'll never really know whether a candidate is truly a candidate or an undercover officer, it is important that you treat everyone the same. Here is the line-up of the common personalities that you may come across and how to deal with each of them in an appropriate manner.

The Show-Off

You can be certain to find a show-off at every cabin crew interview. You will recognise him or her by their showy, self-absorbed and obnoxious attitude. While this personality type is easily annoying, the truth is that these individuals tend to be deeply insecure. They brag about their own achievements through fear that nobody will otherwise notice. Be kind and sincerely acknowledge their efforts when appropriate. This will demonstrate that you are not easily antagonised, but are also sensitive to the feelings of others.

The Rival

In playing the part of the rival, the officer will demonstrate a very competitive streak, which puts you and everyone else as their competition and a threat to their success. They will attempt to make you feel inferior in order to throw you of guard. With these personality types, it is important to be friendly, but respectful of their space. Remember, competitive people are passionate, driven and innovative, so embrace these positive traits and don't let their feeling of superiority run you down.

The Gossip-Monger

Gossipmongers like to point out other people's flaws or failures in an attempt to feel superior. This personality type is a favourite amongst officers because it can reveal a great deal about a candidate. Are you passive or assertive? Do you engage in gossip or show disapproval?

The best defence in this scenario is to first neutralise the negative comment by pointing out a positive and contrary opinion and then attempting to change the subject. If you have a tenacious officer, they may continue to press. In this instance, it would be wise to respectfully state that you would rather not discuss the merits of others, as it is not your place to do so. This honest approach should dissolve any further discussion on the subject. Failing that, it would be best to take your leave immediately.

The Think-They-Know-It-All

Know-it-all's have an attitude of superiority and like to think they are experts in everything. In conversation, they are arrogant and condescending and openly disregard the opinion of others. Remain cordial and patient and, whatever you do, don't be drawn into a debate, become critical or impatient. If the so called expert becomes overbearing or it is obvious that they are not an expert at all, you assertiveness skill s may be being tested, so you may tactfully and respectfully state the facts as you perceive them.

The Overly Anxious

The part of an anxious candidate is a prime opportunity to observe your patience and sensitivity. Experiencing a heightened level of anxiety is very traumatic and paralysing, so be friendly and supportive with these individuals. Offer words of encouragement, but don't place too much focus on their anxiety. Rather, try to break their state by asking questions about things they enjoy and that make them feel relaxed. You could ask them about their hobbies or desires.

The Negativist

Ah, the negativist. There's always one in every crowd and officers love to use this one to gauge a candidate's ability to remain positive under pressure. At best, negativists are very annoying. At worst, they will drain every ounce of energy and motivation from your body. If your attempts to motivate or encourage these people fall flat, remain positive and try to distance yourself as much as possible. If this is not possible, detach yourself from their words and stay focused on your own positive energy.

The Aggressor

Passive aggressors are covert and manipulative. They disguise their attacks as constructive criticism or harmless jokes so that, in the instance that they are confronted, they can deny any wrong doing. If you find yourself under attack from these predators, you may ask questions that will temp them into the open, such as: "Forgive me, but that sounded like a disrespectful comment, was it?" In the worst case, you may try to distance yourself.

If the aggressor is more openly disrespectful and disparaging, the best approach is to remain calm and composed, listen attentively and without interruption until they have finished. A counter attack will only reflect badly on you, so resist the tendency to fight back. Instead, acknowledge their opinion and then voice your own in a respectful manner or simply remove yourself from them as much as possible.

The Open Book

If an individual airs all their dirty laundry to you, revealing all sorts of personal hardships, it could be that they are looking for a reciprocal response. You may demonstrate empathy for their situation, but avoid getting drawn too deeply into conversation about of their hardship and avoid revealing any of your own. Changing the subject and pointing out the positive is always the best course of action.

The Unusual Suspects

The aforementioned scenarios are rather obvious, so they are generally easier to contend with. Where the traps really lie are in those personalities, which are not negative at all. In fact, it is the positive personalities, such as those in the following scenarios, which will often catch a candidate off guard. Because these personality types are friendly, approachable and easy to get on with, it is very easy to lose yourself in conversation with such individuals. It is with these personality types that you really need to be on your guard. So lets take a look at the contenders.

The Extrovert

Extroverts are very sociable creatures and thrive on interaction. They are comfortable speaking to large audiences, are very open with their thoughts and feelings, and take an enthusiastic approach to most activities. This personality type is easy to get caught up in dialogue with, so you need to be extra cautious about the information you openly reveal when in their intoxicating presence. Enjoy the buzz they create and allow their enthusiasm to radiate through you and if you have an introverted tendency, just bide you time and make an effort to enjoy their vibrant presence.

The Entertainer

Just like extroverts, entertainers are sociable, talkative and very energetic people. They love to be the centre of attention and often have an infectious personality. It is very easy to like the entertainer as they have a very down to earth and friendly attitude. When interacting with an entertainer, avoid being overly serious and just allow their positive energy to flow through you. An officer will use this type of personality to lure you into a false sense of security, so beware.

The Model

In using the term 'model', I am not referring to looks. Rather, I am referring to those candidates who seem to be models of perfection. They appear to say and do all the right things, seemingly without a care or worry in the world. They naturally exude charisma and confidence, and have a magnetic personality. Officers will use this personality type for two reasons. The first is so officers can gauge other candidates reactions to their presence, and two, they will be providing an example for others to learn from. In observing these candidates, examine what makes them appear perfect and be appreciative of those traits.

The Leader

Natural leaders are instantly recognisable by their innate desire to step up. Their confident, assertive and intelligent character inspires trust in others, while their sensitive, inspiring and sincere side inspires confidence. Officers will often use this approach to test a candidate's ability and willingness to support and encourage their fellow candidates without viewing them as competition. In the presence of a good leader, respect, support and encourage their efforts. Participate and be an active member of their team and you may just join them in the next round.

These are just some of the personality types that you may come across, but there may be many more. So always be on your guard with everyone you come in contact with.

Handling

QUESTIONS & DIALOGUE

Handling a personality type is one thing, but answering their intrusive questions or resisting deadly dialogue is quite another. So here are a few tips that will help you in this most critical part of the process.

Q: So, what do you do for a living?

This question is so common and seemingly innocent that it is easy to get caught out with. If you are between jobs, dislike your current job, or are desperate to find a new job this question can lead to and encourage negative dialogue. When answering this question, just remember to keep the discussion positive and be careful not to reveal too much about your personal circumstances if they are less than ideal.

Q: Don't you just hate interviews?

Let's be honest, unless you are like me and attend them for fun or research purposes, it is unlikely that you will relish attending interviews. However, just as you would attempt to diffuse a negative interview question with a positive response, you should do the same here. So, rather than admit to disliking interviews, you can state that you simply see it as a necessary part of the process in achieving the job that you desire and, therefore, you appreciate its necessity.

Q: This is my seventh attempt. How many interviews have you attended?

If an applicant asks you any questions regarding your previous interview attempts or current interview strategies you really must not divulge such information. You could attempt to change the subject in the first instance or, failing that, you may be polite and state that you would rather not focus on the past as you are trying to remain focused on the present.

Q: I had to take a sickie to attend this damn thing, how did you manage to take time off?

This question has many motives and your best response is a neutral one. Simply state that you have been preparing for this day for some time and have allocated time into your schedule for its purpose. There is no need to say any more.

Q: I want this job because ... What about you?

An honest and passionate response to this question will surely set you apart, so by all means share this passion if you feel it is appropriate to do so. Clearly the lure of travel is not appropriate, but you may be surprised that some individuals still use this line.

Q: My daughter decided to misbehave, today of all days. Do you have children?

This question is trying to elicit further information about your personal life. Rather than divulge this personal information you may choose to ignore it and just empathise by saying " Kids sure do pick their moments don't they? But you've got to love them". You may then attempt to change the subject. Asking follow-up questions will only encourage further dialogue and you will want to avoid this where possible.

Q: Why do we have to sing and dance? Surely this isn't part of our job description

This comment is trying to entice you to speak negatively about a task. This doesn't necessarily have to be about singing and dancing, it could be about any task. Even if you share their viewpoint, remain positive by indicating that you find such challenges fun and are eager to get involved. Nobody will know how you really feel if you don't share it.

Artful dodging

If you encounter a tenacious officer who continues to press your buttons or if you feel backed into a corner at any time, there may be no alternative but to relieve yourself from their presence as soon as possible.

In planning your escape, you will want to make it as seamless and natural as possible so that you can avoid, or at least minimise, causing offence. You could do this during a task or a session break when the individual is conversing with other candidates. This will make it less likely that your disappearance will be noticed. Whatever you do, be sure to have a plan in mind or you risk being left alone and looking like a lost puppy: This surely won't do you any favours.

Sure there will be a risk that a real candidate may feel insulted or upset if they catch on to your disappearing act, however, if your escape is truly justified, then such candidates are not worthy of your concern as they will only bring you down. On the other hand, an officer will at least recognise your ability to distance yourself from negative situations.

PRACTICAL
TASKS

Bridging the Gap

Duration: 30 Minutes

Instructions

With the materials provided, design and construct a bridge which strong enough to support a roll of sticky tape.

Materials

- » 5 sheets of A4 paper
- » A pair of scissors
- » 1 Metre length of sticky tape
- » 4 Drinking straws
- » 1 Metre length of string
- » 2 Elastic bands

Let Me Entertain You Duration: 40 Minutes

Instructions

As you reach cruising altitude, you discover that the in flight entertainment system has failed.

To ensure the passengers are entertained for the duration of the four hour flight, design a game concept and present it to the rest of the group in a teaching style.

Advertising Space

Duration: 40 Minutes

Instructions

Emirates has secured a prime time radio spot and needs a new commercial campaign.

Using the team's collective knowledge of the airline, create a compelling commercial that will attract new customers.

The final broadcast must be no more than 45 seconds in length, and each team member must have an active role in the final presentation.

Points to Consider

This activity will highlight your knowledge of the airline, so be ready with plenty of input from your research.

Designer Wear

Duration: 45 Minutes

Instructions

Emirates is looking to update its image and needs new designs for its cabin crew uniform.

Consider the existing design and come up with a new or modified concept.

Points to Consider

During this task, be mindful of what is considered appropriate to the culture.

Also, take inspiration from the current design as it provides valuable insight into what the airline considers to be appropriate.

Just when the caterpillar thought the world was over, it became a butterfly

- Proverb

GROUP
DISCUSSIONS

Survivor

Instructions

Your flight is scheduled to land in Los Angeles, however, due to mechanical difficulties the plane was forced to land on a remote island.

During landing, much of the equipment aboard was damaged, but 10 items have been recovered intact. Your task is to rank them in terms of their importance for your crew.

Items

» A box of matches

» 15 feet of nylon rope

» 5 gallons of water

» Signal flares

» A self inflating life raft

» A magnetic compass

» First aid kit

» A fruit basket

» A tub of dry milk powder

» A shotgun

Day Trip

Duration: 30 Minutes

Instructions

You have been given the responsibility for arranging a day trip for 15 disabled children. Discuss where you would take the children, what activities you would have arranged and why.

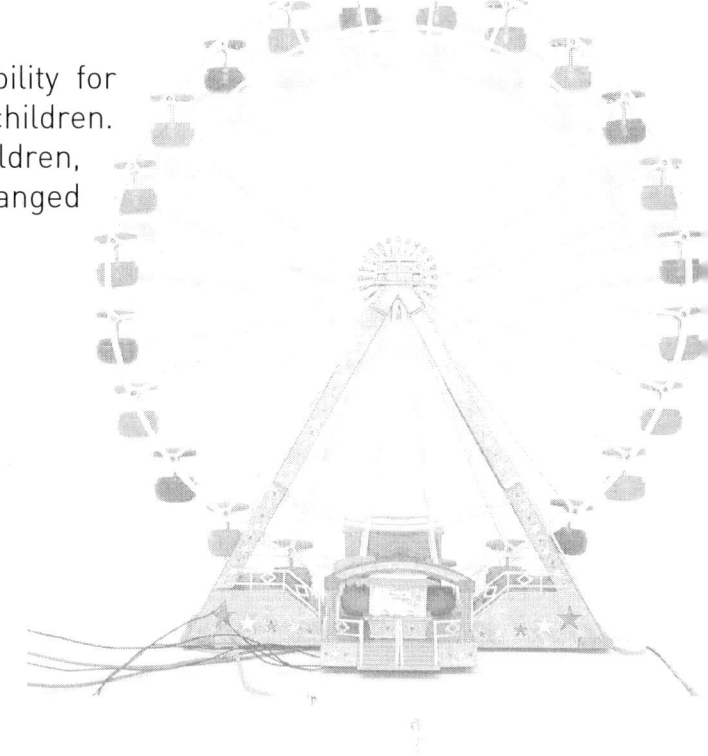

Options

- » Theme park
- » Museum
- » White water rafting
- » Trip on the Orient Express
- » Water Park
- » Safari
- » Art gallery
- » Scenic helicopter ride

Points to Consider

In this instance, the children in question are disabled. So, certain activities will not be appropriate, while others may not sufficiently capture the children's interest. It is important to gain a balance between having fun and being safe.

" Too many of us are not living our dreams because we are living our fears "

- Les Brown

ROLE PLAY
SCENARIOS

Role-play

SCENARIOS

Role-play scenarios may be performed with other candidates as a pair or within a group, or they may be performed one on one with an assessor.

The scenarios will bear some relation to the demands of the job and are likely to include:

Intoxicated passenger	Disorderly behaviour
Terrorist threat	Disruptive child
Toilet smoker	Abusive behaviour
Fearful passenger	Passenger complaint

The assessors don't expect you to know the answer to every possible scenario they introduce. They simply want to see how you react in challenging situations. So, when taking part in any role play scenario, use the following guidelines:

- Be proactive and do your best to resolve the situation using your initiative
- Remain calm and composed
- Be direct and assertive
- Immerse yourself into the role
- Take each scenario seriously
- Devise a plan and follow it as much as possible

Here are some pointers to help you deal with some common scenarios:

Complaint

In the case of a passenger complaint, it is important that you listen to their concern without interruption. Ask questions, where appropriate, to clarify their concerns and show empathy towards their situation. If the facts warrant it, apologise for the situation, explain what action you intend to take and thank them for bringing the matter to your attention.

Fearful passenger

If a passenger is fearful of flying, be considerate of their feelings. Use a gentle and calm tone to talk them through the flight and reassure them of any sounds or sensations they may experience. Let the passenger know where you can be found and show them the call bell.

Intoxicated passenger

Offer the passenger a cup of tea or coffee and don't provide any more alcoholic drinks. You could also encourage the passenger to eat some food. Remain calm towards the passenger, but be direct and assertive in your approach. If you feel it appropriate, inform your senior and seek assistance from other crewmembers.

The group tasks and discussion are updated regularly, so the above examples are only for demonstration purposes. In any case, remember that the outcome of the task is irrelevant. Always be mindful of your behaviour and how you are being percieved by those around you.

" If you do what you've
always done, you'll get
what you've always gotten "

- Anthony Robbins

THE
TESTING STAGE

Important tips

AND ADVICE

When carrying out any kind of test, it is important that you read the questions through fully and make sure you completely understand what is being asked before attempting to answer. Nothing looks more sloppy or unprepared than handing in a test sheet with scribbles and corrections all over it.

Begin by going through the test sheet and completing all the questions you find easy. With this strategy, you can be confident that you have at least answered as many questions as possible should you get stuck on other trickier questions for an extended period of time.

It is also a good idea to go through a final check when you are finished to ensure that no mistakes have been made inadvertently. If you have sufficient time, you may mark your answers in pencil first, so that when you are completing your final check any mistakes can be easily rectified.

Psychometric

AND PERSONALITY PROFILE

It is believed that psychometric tests provide a clear assessment of a candidate's ability to carry out a job, and whether the character of an individual will complement the current working environment.

Psychometric testing helps to build a profile of characteristics, behavioural style and personality. For example, how does a candidate interact with others? How do they react within a certain situation? Is a candidate able to do the job for which they have applied? Is a candidate a natural leader with individual initiative? Etc...

The reason Emirates use psychometric testing during the recruitment process is because they have a clear idea of the sort of person they are looking to recruit. If you are not the sort of person Emirates are looking for, then you are unlikely to be happy in the job in the long term, no matter how superficially attractive it may be.

Trying to beat the system

When approaching a psychometric test, it is important to answer the questions as honestly as possible. It is understandable that you will want to create a favourable impression, and you may even be tempted to tailor your answers according to what you think Emirates want to hear, but falsifying your answers will only lead to unnatural and inconsistent results.

Moreover, the correct answer may not always be obvious, as they are often written in a way that makes it difficult to distinguish. Take the following question for instance: 'I prefer to work independently, rather than in a team'.

On first impressions, disagreeing with this answer may seem like the obvious choice, after all teamwork is an important aspect of the cabin crew role, right? However, if you think about the question from an alternative perspective, it may be that Emirates are trying to ascertain if you are able and willing to use your own initiative, another important quality. So, what about a middle of the road answer? One or two middle of the road answers are acceptable, however, too many will make you appear indecisive and unsure, and you many not reach the minimum required score. So what is the best answer? It's simple, the best answer is the one that is honest.

A decision-making tool

The psychometric test is no doubt a valuable assessment tool, however, it is not an instant pass or fail decision-making tool. It is used simply as a supplement what the assessors have already observed about you and your involvement during the assessment day. If you answered the above example in the affirmative, and you also demonstrated the ability to work well within a team environment, both aspects will be taken into consideration.

An example

The tests you are given will be updated often, however, here is a basic example of how a psychometric assessment is generally carried out and the types of questions you can expect to be asked...

Mark each of the following statements on a scale of 1 to 5 where:
1 = Strongly agree   2 = Agree   3 = Not sure   4 = Disagree   5 = Strongly disagree

1	At work, I like to be told exactly what to do	1	2	3	4	5
2	If you want something done properly, you have to do it yourself	1	2	3	4	5
3	We often need help and advice from our superiors	1	2	3	4	5
4	I find it easy to relax after a hard day	1	2	3	4	5
5	I would like to win the lottery and retire early	1	2	3	4	5
6	Most people are honest	1	2	3	4	5
7	I have a career development plan in mind	1	2	3	4	5
8	I believe that the end justifies the means	1	2	3	4	5
9	Would you prefer to be an author (1) or an actor (2)	1	2	?		
10	I can achieve anything if I try hard enough	1	2	3	4	5
11	I enjoy meeting new people	1	2	3	4	5
12	I get bored doing repetitive tasks	1	2	3	4	5
13	I often lose my temper when I am frustrated	1	2	3	4	5
14	Who do you admire more – Madonna (1) or Mahatma Gandhi (2)	1	2	?		
15	I need alcohol to give me confidence around other people	1	2	3	4	5
16	I prefer working independently rather than in a team	1	2	3	4	5
17	I fall sick often	1	2	3	4	5
18	I always think before I act	1	2	3	4	5
19	I respect my superiors decisions even if I don't agree	1	2	3	4	5
20	I knew what career I wanted when I left school	1	2	3	4	5
21	Worrying keeps me awake at night	1	2	3	4	5
22	I am often lost for words when meeting people for the first time	1	2	3	4	5
23	I feel dissatisfied with my career progress to date	1	2	3	4	5
24	Are you more introvert (1) or extrovert (2)	1	2	?		
25	I often feel overwhelmed	1	2	3	4	5
26	I enjoy challenges	1	2	3	4	5
27	I make mistakes when I rush	1	2	3	4	5
28	I have an active social life	1	2	3	4	5
29	I sometimes feel depressed with my life	1	2	3	4	5
30	Do you prefer using the stairs (1) or an escalator (2)	1	2	?		

31	I feel confident about my future	1 2 3 4 5
32	I plan activities rather than just going ahead and doing it	1 2 3 4 5
33	I can't work with people I don't like	1 2 3 4 5
34	I listen politely to people with whom I deeply disagree	1 2 3 4 5
35	I find it difficult to bounce back after disappointment	1 2 3 4 5
36	Do you prefer to work with your hands (1) or your brain (2)	1 2 ?
37	I value my reputation for straight talking	1 2 3 4 5
38	When I worry, I bottle it up inside	1 2 3 4 5
39	I need others to motivate me	1 2 3 4 5
40	I can work on my own initiative	1 2 3 4 5
41	I am easily stressed	1 2 3 4 5
42	Are you more productive in the morning (1) or in the evening (2)	1 2 ?
43	I would make a good salesperson	1 2 3 4 5
44	I tire easily	1 2 3 4 5
45	I stand up for what I believe	1 2 3 4 5
46	I sometimes cut corners to get a job done quicker	1 2 3 4 5
47	I would like to be somebody else	1 2 3 4 5
48	Would you rather sit and read a book (1) or go for a walk (2)	1 2 ?
49	I sometimes lie to get what I want	1 2 3 4 5
50	I am a good leader	1 2 3 4 5
51	I take criticism personally	1 2 3 4 5
52	I am a fast learner	1 2 3 4 5
53	Is it more important to be truthful (1) or tactful (2)	1 2 ?
54	I feel most relaxed in my own company	1 2 3 4 5
55	Do you prefer to talk (1) or listen (2)	1 2 ?
56	I remain calm under pressure	1 2 3 4 5
57	I am often late arriving at work	1 2 3 4 5
58	People respect my opinions	1 2 3 4 5
59	I would leave work immediately if a family member became ill	1 2 3 4 5
60	I am confident when addressing a group	1 2 3 4 5

English

COMPREHENSION

The ability to speak and comprehend English is essential for the role of cabin crew and your English proficiency will be observed and evaluated throughout the course of the assessment. If English isn't your native language, you will also be required to pass an English comprehension assessment.

The 'Test of English as a Foreign Language' (TOEFL) system is used for this purpose, and I recommend seeking further study in this area if you have concerns in your ability. There are several books I recommend for this purpose, and these are noted within the Bibliography section at the back of the book.

For the Emirates comprehension test, you can expect to be assessed on the following four areas:

- Listening
- Reading
- Writing
- Speaking

These skills can be assessed within three modes of communication:

· Interpersonal (involving two-way interactive communication)
· Interpretive (relating to the understanding of spoken or written language)
· Presentational (involving creating spoken or written communication)

Performance on assessment tasks will be evaluated by how well you understand (comprehension) and can be understood (comprehensibility). The evaluation considers language knowledge, the appropriate use of communication strategies, and the application of cultural knowledge to enhance communication.

FINAL INTERVIEW

PART 5

Contents
Of this Session

"The future belongs to those who believe in the beauty of their dreams

- *Eleanor Roosevelt*

WHAT TO
EXPECT

What to expect

Congratulations if you have made it through to the final interview. Having assessed your involvement and performance during the group sessions, the recruiters have clearly observed qualities in your character that they admire, and would now like to explore your motives further. So revel in the success you have achieved to this point, and be ready to close out this process.

During the final interview, the recruiters will seek to explore your motives for applying to Emirates and your desire for pursuing a career as cabin crew. Moreover, they will seek to gather information about your work history, character and work ethic to determine whether you will fit the job and airline.

To ease you into the interview process, and make you feel more relaxed, the recruiters will typically open the session with questions about you and your background. They will then seek to explore your motivation for applying to Emirates and making a career change. Questions such as "Why do you want to work for us?" and "Why do you want to be cabin crew?" are common at this stage.

With the interview thoroughly under way, the recruiters will want to determine whether you possess the skills and experience necessary for the position. Here you can expect more probing situational and behavioural questions, such as "When have you handled a customer complaint?" and "Describe a time when you failed to communicate effectively".

Although there appears to be no typical duration for panel interviews, you can expect a baseline time of at least 20 minutes, to upwards of 1 hour or more. In either case, the duration has no bearing on your ultimate success; so do not overly concern yourself with this aspect. An interview lasting just 20 minutes doesn't indicate a failure, just as an interview in excess of 1 hour does not indicate success.

Icebreaker

OR DEAL-BREAKER

The interviewers will have several tricks up their sleeves to extract information during the course of the interview, but it is during the pre-interview 'ice breaking' session that you must be extra cautious.

During the first few moments of an interview it is only natural that most candidates will be feeing nervous, and it is under the rush of adrenaline that candidates are most likely to reveal too much information. It is also during these first few moments that candidates get caught off guard because they expect to be softly broken into the interview before the interrogation actually begins. Interviewers use this assumption to their advantage.

Personnel are trained to use trick questions, in the form of icebreakers, to get candidates to inadvertently volunteer sensitive and personal information about their circumstances and background. They will use friendly manipulation and small talk to lull candidates into a false sense of security. Under these conditions, they are able to extract information very easily from unsuspecting candidates.

So, whatever happens and however relaxed the interviewers attempt to make you feel, remember that you are being assessed and you need to keep your whit's about you.

Meet the

RECRUITMENT TEAM

Typically, there will be two or three official recruitment officers present during the final interview. These officers may be HR personnel, or they may be working senior crewmembers. Either way, you can be sure that they are experienced recruitment professionals.

To successfully interact with these recruitment personnel, it is important to understand their styles and be prepared to deal with them accordingly. Within a cabin crew interview setting, you will typically encounter two dominant styles of interviewer. I call these: The interrogation experts and the guardian angels.

The interrogation expert

Interrogation experts believe that candidates will only show their true personalities while under intense pressure. As a result, they adopt a direct and intimidating style of questioning and will cross-examine every answer you provide. During this onslaught of questioning, they will be observing your ability to remain calm and think on your feet. So, approach their questions in a calm and confident manner and be direct and succinct in your response.

The guardian angel

Guardian angels will attempt to relieve the pressure of the atmosphere by engaging in friendly conversation. While their relaxed and friendly style can be a welcome relief, unsuspecting candidates may become overly casual and reveal more than is appropriate. Caution is therefore advised to avoid being culled by these friendly tactics. You certainly don't to want to appear rigid, but you do need to be mindful of who you are talking to and remain professional.

What assessors

ARE REALLY LOOKING FOR

Recruiters understand that you will not be able to answer every question perfectly, and they also understand that you may not know the answer to each question that is asked. What they do expect and what they are invested in is how you respond to certain lines of questioning and how you conduct yourself. As such, their line of questioning will be designed to reveal your ability to:

- Listen actively
- Express yourself articulately, confidently and professionally
- Answer questions logically and concisely
- Remain calm under pressure

Some of the questions are designed specifically to throw you off guard, to see how you react to the pressure. With these sorts of questions, the interviewers are not necessarily looking for a perfect answer, but they are looking for a quick and well-prepared response.

They will also use several tactics to elicit a negative reaction or encourage you to reveal more than you should. This may be through the use of the silent treatment (as discussed in part 1), or through a line of questioning that is designed to keep you from knowing the correct answer. They will use trick questions, behavioural questions and even trick questions in the guise of a positive question, all in an attempt to rattle you and make you fall apart during the process.

Ultimately, it is important to remember that the recruiters are looking to hire positive people, so it is important to remain calm and composed throughout the interview and never show that you have been flustered.

The lull of reciprocation

Following on from the friendly interviewer routine is the lull of reciprocation tactic. This tactic is probably one of the sneakiest because it is very easy to be taken in if you are unprepared. Here's how it works:

You enter the interviewer's office and the officer casually begins to open dialogue with some small talk about their children, or complains about their knee as they struggle to take their seat. Harmless? Unfortunately not! The purpose of this dialogue is to encourage a reciprocal response. For those candidates who are parents themselves, it is only natural that they too will begin to talk about your own children in response to such a comment. Or if a candidate is facing health struggles of their own, they may feel compelled to share out of empathy or politeness. 3178

These are just two examples, but there could be many more related to age, marital status, or your employment history. The list could go on.

Reciprocal remarks are quite acceptable in a social setting, but are completely inappropriate during a formal interview. So if you ever find yourself faced with this situation, the best approach is to respond with a question. For instance, in response to a comment about their children, you could ask, 1405 "How old is your son/daughter?" Likewise, in response to any statements relating to health, you could simply state "oh dear, I'm sorry to hear of your knee trouble. How did you hurt it?" These responses maintain a friendly connection, without giving anything away. In most cases, this will be sufficient to move the interview along.

MISERY LOVES COMPANY

The Awkward
SILENCE

One of the most common interview traps you will encounter is the silent treatment. With this trick, the interviewer will respond to your answer with a blank stare and a deadening silence. This trick is so incredibly effective because most candidates are so intimidated by silence that they will often rush to fill the void.

Rather than see the silence as just a pause for thought, many candidates will view the silence as an indication that they have just goofed up in some way. It is in their haste to justify and recover their answer that they then volunteer irrelevant or damaging information, often appearing flustered and knocking themselves out of contention.

The point of using silence is to see how you respond to stress, therefore, whenever you are confronted with silence, the best strategy is to remain silent yourself. If the silence persists after 5-10 seconds, you can proceed to ask "is there anything I can add to clarify this point?" or "Did I answer the question fully enough?" These questions will demonstrate that you are not intimidated by silence or stress and will put the responsibility clearly back onto the interviewer. If there is something troubling him or her, this will encourage disclosure and an appropriate opportunity for you to reiterate.

The friendly
INTERVIEWER ROUTINE

The friendly interviewer routine is one that catches even the most seasoned candidates off guard. You enter the interview room and are surprised to discover that you are greeted by a warm and friendly welcome. The interviewer chats openly about all sorts of things, almost as if you are just catching up with an old friend. They make you feel at ease and, as you feel like you are starting to make a connection with this friendly individual, you suddenly find yourself letting your guard down.

Maybe you feel that you've created some sort of friendship. Maybe this interviewer is looking to help you get a job. Wrong! Interviewers are trained to be enthusiastic and friendly representatives of the airline, and it is this friendly approach that lulls candidates into a false sense of security. Under these relaxed conditions the interviewer is able to get a better sense of who you really are, and before you know it you begin revealing sensitive information about your home life, financial problems, health, former employer and challenges you are facing. By the time you realise that you've said too much, it's already too late.

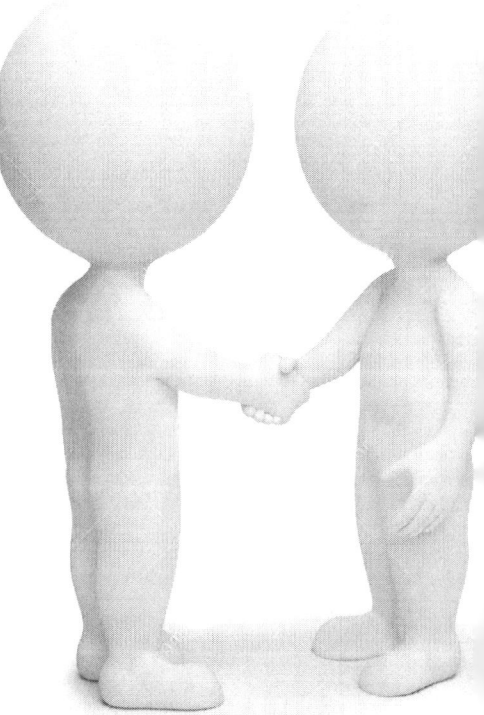

Whenever you meet the interviewer for the first time, it is important not to be taken in by this friendly approach. You certainly don't to want to appear rigid, by any means, but you do need to be mindful of who you are talking to and remain professional.

The guise
OF A POSITIVE QUESTION

Lets say that partly through the interview when the recruiter asks how soon you can start. This is a simple question and one that has positive connotations. Unfortunately, this is an example of a trick question, which has been disguised as a positive one. When candidates hear this question, the natural response is one of excitement as they feel they are being offered the job. Without much thought, they begin to express a willingness to get started straight away.

The problem with this response is that if you are in employment your answer indicates that you are not willing to provide appropriate notice, and therefore will not be fulfilling obligations to your current employer. This surely does not work in your favour.

The best answer in response to this question is to affirm, "I have the energy and enthusiasm to start straight away. All I need is two week's notice for my current employer".

The abrupt end

The abrupt end is just how it sounds. All of the sudden, as if from out of nowhere, the interviewer declares an end to the interview. They show you to the door and thank you for your time. What should you make of this?

This sort of abrupt end is very similar to the silent treatment trick, in the sense that the interviewer is seeking your reaction to the stress of uncertainty. At this point, the formal interview really is over, however, your assessment is not. Your reaction will be observed very closely as you depart from the room and exit the premises. Do you remain composed or do you storm out of the building in defiance? Do you acknowledge the receptionist on your departure or simply ignore them?

As soon as you realise that the interview has reached its conclusion, regardless of what has happened and how you are feeling, it is important to depart gracefully for that final lasting impression.

Gather your belongings and, as you rise from your seat, straighten your clothing. Upon standing, thank the interviewer for his or her time and offer a final handshake. Make your way towards the door, stop and turn, and say your final thank you before making your exit. As you approach the front desk, acknowledge the receptionist with a sincere thank you and continue on your way. Only when you are clear of the area can you let out the scream of defiance, not before.

Does this abrupt end mean that you have been unsuccessful? Absolutely not! In fact, if handled well it could mark your success.

A WINNING
APPROACH

Answers

AS EASY AS **A.B.C**

When preparing your answers to traditional questions, keep the A.B.C formula in mind.

Answer

Make your answer concise by answering the question directly

Back it up

Back up your answer with solid facts. This will add a lot of weight to any statements made.

Conclude

The conclusion allows you to expand on your skills and what you can offer the airline

Consider the following example:

What is your best attribute?

Answer:
"As you will have observed during the group assessments, I am a very welcoming and social individual who interacts well with others, and readily adapts to new people and environments."

Back it up:
"In fact, my previous supervisor also picked up on these attributes and often asked me to carry out the client shampoo because she knew I would make the clients feel welcome and relaxed"

Conclude:
"I am confident that this aspect of my character will enable me to perform the job to the same high standard that exists currently within the airline"

A.C.T

ON NEGATIVE QUESTIONS

Negative questions can be better approached using the A.C.T formula.

 ## Attack

By attacking the question head on, not only do you avoid being alienated by the question, it also allows you to swiftly move on and add clarity to your response.

 ## Clarify

This is your opportunity to add any clarity and facts that may support or justify your answer.

 ## Turn

Now turn the focus away from the initial negative question to focus on the positive outcome of the experience.

Consider the following example:

What is your greatest weakness?

Attack:
"I recognise that my leadership ability is a potential area of improvement"

Clarify:
"Which is why I am actively working on developing this area further through a part time training course at my local college"

Turn:
"Although I am still learning, I see constant improvement in my capabilities when being faced with leadership tasks and I am confident that I will continue to learn and grow with experience"

Winning answers

WITH THE **S.A.R.R** FORMULA

When preparing your examples to competency-based questions, the S.A.R.R formula can help you structure your response.

 Situation

Briefly describe the challenge, problem, or task

A Action

Describe what you did and how you did it

R Result

Describe the outcome and how your actions affected the outcome or the people involved

R Reflection

Elaborate on what you learned from the experience and whether you would do things differently in the future.

Consider the following example:

When have you used your initiative to solve a problem?

Situation:
"I was in the staff room during my lunch break, and I could hear a lot of noise coming from inside the salon. I went to investigate and two, very bored, little girls confronted me. I could sense that their excitement was causing a disruption and inconvenience"

Action:
"I immediately took the initiative and attempted to occupy them by offering to plait their hair while they made bracelets from some hair beads. Their eyes sparkled with excitement and I was able to keep them occupied for the remainder of their visit"

Result:
"We had lots of fun and, while the calm was restored, the stylist was able to complete the clients' treatment"

Reflection:
"I felt really pleased that with just a little extra effort, I had made such a big difference"

Probing with

FOLLOW-UP QUESTIONS

Follow up questions are either used to verity the viability of your answer, or to tempt negative information into the open. So it is important to have examples ready to back up any statements made.

Prepare to be asked:

- What did you learn from the experience?
- What specifically did you say?
- How did you feel?
- Would you do anything differently?
- How did they react?
- What other options did you consider?
- Why did you decide to take the action that you did?
- You mentioned ... Tell me more about that.
- How did you retain your composure?
- Can you give me an example of that?
- Can you be more specific about...?

The constant

INTERRUPTION

In an attempt to throw you off, the recruiter may even interrupt your responses with supplementary probing questions.

Take a look at the following example.

When have you disagreed with a colleague?

Candidate
"Working in a creative environment with other highly skilled professionals, it was natural that we had the occasional clash of ideas."

Recruiter
"Please can you elaborate further?"

Candidate
"We would sometimes have a clash of ideas based around our individual preference towards certain products, styles, magazines or equipment. Although, any disagreements we did have were relatively minor and insignificant."

Recruiter
"What would you consider minor and insignificant?"

Candidate

"Our debates were never confrontational, and they never interfered with our work in any way. In fact, some disagreements were quite educational."

Recruiter

"Educational?"

Candidate

"Yes, some very interesting views emerged from these debates which sometimes resulted in people, including myself, having a slight change in perspective."

Recruiter

"Can you tell me about a change you had in perspective following such a debate?"

...

It is important to answer the questions without demonstrating any frustration or resentment, Once you have answered the quesiton, smile and get straight back on point.

Seven

HEAVENLY VIRTUES

 ## Stay focused

If you fail to control your internal dialogue you will not only lose your composure, but you also risk misunderstanding the question. Remain completely focused on what the recruiter is saying and focus on giving the best possible answer. Concerns about how you look and the outcome should be postponed until after the interview.

 ## Listen actively

Although you should never interrupt the recruiter, you shouldn't listen in total silence either. Instead, use verbal feedback cues to indicate that you are listening and that you understand. This will encourage the recruiter to continue. Some verbal feedback signals include: "I see", "Yes", "I understand", "Sure".

Inject personality

Injecting passion and personality into your answers will add life and sincerity. It will also keep the recruiters interested in what you are saying.

4 Be concise

If an answer is too long-winded, the recruiter will become complacent. Keeping your answers short and concise will retain their attention.

5 Vary your voice

Varying your tone, pitch, volume and pace will eliminate monotone and make it enjoyable for the recruiters to listen to. Slowing your pace slightly will also add clarity.

6 Be positive

A positive spirit will reflect well on your character and allow the recruiters to warm towards you. So, be enthusiastic about the interview and the job, and speak respectfully about your previous employers and positions.

7 Maintain eye contact

Regular, strong eye contact will give the impression of someone who is honest and confident. Where there is more than one recruitment officer, you should maintain eye contact with the person who asks you the question while occasionally engaging eye contact with the second recruiter.

Seven

DEADLY SINS

1 Controlling

Trying to lead or control the conversation will appear arrogant and disrespectful. Ask questions when appropriate opportunities arise, but allow the recruiter to do his or her job.

2 Interrupting

Interruptions are rude and disrespectful to the speaker. So, unless absolutely necessary, you should allow the recruiter to finish speaking before responding or asking for clarification.

3 Lying

If you lie, there will be a very good chance that you will be caught out when the recruiters probe into your answers with follow up questions. If this happens, you could end up looking rather silly and, worse still, any chance of being offered the job will be ruined.

Talking incessantly

It's easy to talk too much when nervous, however, it is important to remember that interviews are two-way exchanges. A moment of silence, while it might seem awkward to you, lets the recruiter know that you are done and allows them to move the interview along.

 # Being negative

Making negative remarks or exhibiting frustration over tasks, peers, other airlines or previous employers, no matter how harmless it may seem, will raise serious concerns about your attitude and ethics.

 # Overusing filler words

The useless and annoying verbal mannerisms "you know," "like," "in other words," "kind of," "ummm," and "anyways." should be avoided at all costs. Besides making you sound unprofessional, they also detract attention from your message.

 # Unprepared or unnecesary questions

To stand out as an informed and competent applicant, your questions should reflect that you have researched the airline and the position. Asking questions that have already been addressed within the airline's literature will make you appear unprepared and incompetent. Likewise, asking questions that are based on money and benefits will make you appear selfishly motivated and give a negative impression about your motives for the position and/or the airline.

Avoid robotic

FLAT AND BORING ANSWERS

In preparing for the final interview, it may make sense to memorise some of your answers. Unfortunately, trying to memorise an answer for every scenario will only work against you. Not only do you run the risk of sounding like a robot, with a boring and flat delivery, but you also risk forgetting your answers and appearing flustered as you try to recall the information.

Rather than memorising your answers, make a list of key points and try to remember those instead. Key points are much easier to remember than lengthy sentences and will allow you to create a genuine and spontaneous answer based around that point.

Another technique, that is highly effective and advantageous, is to prepare through actual practice. Whether that is through a role play with a friend or family member, the use of a camcorder or through attending mock interviews with other airlines, practice will allow you to feel much more confident and natural when you do the real thing.

Demonstrate respect for the recruiter

It is important to be observant and sense when the interviewer has heard enough about a particular point. Many candidates go off on a tangent when they get into the swing of the interview, and neglect to notice that the interviewer wants to move on. To demonstrate your respect for the recruiter and his or her time, you could ask "Would you like me to elaborate on that further?" The interviewer will appreciate your effort.

Eek, I don't know the answer

You are not expected to know the answer to every question you are asked. In fact, the interviewer may throw you a curve ball on purpose in order to test you reaction and observe how you respond under the pressure.

Bluffing your way through an answer, for the sake of not wanting to admit that you don't know the answer, will not reflect favourably on you. The interviewer will be much more forgiving if you are honest and admit your lack of knowledge on a particular point.

If you lack relative experience in a particular area, you may consider elaborating on a similar and alternative aspect, or you can take the opportunity to remind them of the skills that you do have and explain how you would tackle the situation if it arose. For instance: "I can't remember ever being in that situation, however, I did face something slightly similar that I could tell you about?".

Run of the mill clichés wil not cut it

Answers such as "I'm a workaholic" or "I'm a perfectionist" or "I try too hard to please everyone" are tired old cliché's and are simply not going to cut it. While they may be true statements, recruiters are not naive and they certainly will not accept generic responses such as these.

Generic answers will only make you sound just like everyone else and will not do you any favours. You need to be more creative and, more importantly, you need to sound sincere.

SAMPLE

ANSWERS

PART 6

Contents
Of this Session

UNCOVERING
YOUR MOTIVES

Why do you want

TO BECOME CABIN CREW?

In order to stand out and differentiate yourself from the crowd, it is important to provide and honest and passionate response to this question. Think about it, why do you really want the job? Where did the desire come from? Was it a childhood dream, or was it sparked by another interest? A generic response involving the lure of travel and glamour will not be viewed positively. Be unique and be creative.

"As a child, I grew up very close to the airport and was fascinated by aircraft. I always felt a buzz of excitement when planes flew overhead and dreamt of someday working within the airline industry. My first ever flight reinforced this desire further, as the crew onboard showed me around the aircraft and even took me into the cockpit to meet the pilots.

This is where my passion for flying initially began, but it wasn't until I carried out a career suitability test at college that I really started to consider cabin crew as a serious future prospect. The test examined personal attributes, interests and skills, and the final result came back suggesting suitability for the occupation.

After this, I began to carry out further research into the job and, the more I researched, the more I realised that this is a job that is tailored to my personality, skills and experience. It is one I will feel committed to and I am confident that I will be good at."

Why do you
WANT TO WORK FOR EMIRATES?

The interviewer is not interested in what the airline or position can do for you, they are more concerned with what you can bring to them. To make the greatest impact begin with a personal story, but close with a demonstration of your knowledge and fit for the airline. This will make you stand out as an informed and enthusiastic individual who has something to offer.

"My first passenger experience with Emirates was two years ago, on a flight from Dubai to Los Angeles. Although I only flew in economy class, the service on board was so immaculate and welcoming, that I was instantly impressed. Following this experience I became a frequent flyer and, when I decided to apply for this position, I was in no doubt who I want to work for.

Based on the research I've done since, it is apparant that Emirates is an industry leader. This, in addition to the outstanding reputation and positive feedback I have received from other employees, have greatly reinforced my decision to apply.

Not only am I an excellent fit for your corporate culture, but I am confident that my background, skills and experience will be a valuable asset that will allow me to contribute to Emirates' ongoing success."

Have you applied to any other airlines?

"Although it is taking a bit of a risk, I haven't applied to other airlines because I am set on working for Emirates. I wanted to see how my application went with you before I considered other options."

If another airline offered you a job, would you take it?

"Because I am set on making cabin crew my future career, I would have to consider other airlines if I am unsuccessful in my application today. However, I believe I am a good match for Emirates and its corporate culture, so I would be naturally disappointed at this prospect."

Where do you picture yourself in five years?

"I very much hope that I shall be with Emirates in five years time. By which time, I will have made a significant contribution to the airline, will have become an experienced senior member of the cabin crew team, and will be working on new ways to advance my career further."

If offered the job, how long will you stay with us?

"I'm approaching this job with a long term view. I hope to make enough of a contribution the airline, that I can move up through the ranks to become an experienced senior member of the cabin crew team."

KNOWLEDGE
ABOUT THE JOB
AND THE AIRLINE

What do you know

ABOUT THIS JOB?

The recruiters want to know that you understand what the role involves and are not naive about the pressures and demands. Stand out by demonstrating your informed knowledge and research.

"I know that the service we see as passenger's form only a small portion of what actually goes on in the job. With safety being the primary concern, there are procedures and checks which must be constantly and consistently completed. Then, when things go wrong, cabin crew are there to take control. Moreover, it is a constant process of cleaning and preparation, paperwork and stock checks, tending to passenger comfort and being of service. Clearly the profession is a very demanding one, but it is also a very exciting and fulfilling one for the right person, which I do believe I am."

What qualities

ARE NECESSARY FOR CABIN CREW?

The recruiters want to know that you understand what the role involves and what qualities are necessary to perform its tasks. Conclude this answer by acknowledging your skills in relation to the position.

"Cabin crew play a vital role in giving a good impression of the airline as a whole. This means crew members need to have good communication and customer care skills, as well as a friendly and welcoming demeanour.

Because of the importance of safety, it is also important that they have the strength of character to cope with difficult people and situations, in a calm and objective manner.

These are all attributes I possess and have demonstrated throughout the 8 years of my career as a beauty consultant, and are the primary reasons I would complement your existing team."

Do you think

THE ROLE IS A GLAMOROUS ONE?

It is no secret that many candidates are drawn to the superficial lifestyle, travel and glamour associated with the industry. The recruiters are trying to determine your motives for seeking the position, but also want to understand that you are not naive about the real challenges and requirements of the position.

"Having thoroughly researched the position, I am aware that the glamour associated with the role is rather superficial. Sure there are benefits of travel, and the crew certainly do make themselves appear glamorous, but the constant travelling between time zones, the long and tiring shifts, unpredictable schedules and irregular working patterns place tough demands on crew and make the job anything but glamorous."

What do you think

ARE THE DISADVANTAGES OF THE JOB?

To deny the obvious drawbacks of the job will only make you sound naive and unprepared, so be up front about the disadvantages and demonstrate that you have considered these carefully.

"The obvious disadvantages are the flight delays and cancellations that crew experience. While passengers also experience these issues, crew experience those far more often. This makes for very long and tiring shifts, irregular working patterns and unpredictable schedules.

Moreover, the regular crossing between different time zones can take its toll leading to jet lag and fatigue.

Every position holds its own share of percieved disadvantages, so I understand them as a necessary part of the position and will do my best to take proactive measures to avoid or minimise any undue consequences. By applying for this position, I have accepted everything that comes with it."

What do you think are the advantages of this position?

"The randomness and variety of the different crew, passenger profiles, roster structure ,and the challenges of the position itself excite me greatly. They are unique elements that you just don't find in normal nine to five jobs. It's a position I will find rewarding in a number of ways."

What aspects of customer service are most important to our passengers?

"Passengers want to feel comfortable and looked after by the airline and crew. They want to be assured that crew will listen to and answer their questions, and will be friendly and polite in doing so. If crew are not approachable, passengers feel unwelcome and unsure."

What do you think contributes to passenger frustrations?

"Feeling tired from travelling can cause passengers to feel unusually frustrated. Add to this flight delays, long waiting times and space constrictions, and frustration naturally increases. If the passenger is then greeted by seemingly unwelcoming staff, their tension will certainly rise much further."

Why do you think some passengers vent their frustrations on cabin crew?

"In the first instance, cabin crew wear the airline's uniform, thus passengers consider them to be a representative of the airline. Moreover, the passengers spend more time with cabin crew than with any other member of the airline staff, so they simply become an easy target."

What do you know

ABOUT EMIRATES?

This is where your research will pay off handsomely. Demonstrate your enthusiasm by sharing knowledge that will reveal the effort you have taken to learn more about the airline and its operations.

"Emirates began operating in 1985 with just two leased aircraft, serving only 3 destinations -Bombay, Delhi and Karachi. Within its first two years of operation, Emirates had acquired three fully owned aircraft (a Boeing 727 and two Airbus A310-300's) and had expanded its network to include 6 new destinations (Dhaka, Colombo, Cairo, Oman, London, Istanbul and Frankfurt).

The airline now operates more than 220 aircraft, serving over 140 destinations in more than 80 countries on six continents.

As a testament to Emirates excellent standard of service, it has acquired international awards for customer service excellence and even the world's best airline. Emirates is now one of the largest and popular airlines in the world."

How would you

RATE US AGAINST OUR COMPETITORS?

This question can be a tricky one to answer for those who are unprepared. If you read between the lines, you will see that interviewer is seeking to discover your understanding about the airline and its competition.

In answering this question, remain positive by focusing your answer on the advantages of the airline you are applying for and what they do well.

Example 1
"It's so difficult to be objective, and I really don't like to slight your competition."

Example 2
"My experiences with each of the airlines I have flown with have all been good, and I never had a problem or cause for complaint. An advantage of Emirates, however, is the attentiveness of the crew. They really take care of all their passengers and do everything to make the flight as pleasant as possible. I have always been made to feel welcome on board your flights, even in economy.

Any airline can fly a customer from A to B, but it is the attentiveness of the crew that can mean the difference between a good experience and a pleasurable one. I can only hope I will be so lucky as to work for an airline who cares so deeply about its passengers as the Emirates crew certainly do."

Have you ever flown with us?

"Yes, I have had the fortunate opportunity to fly with Emirates on several occasions now. With the attentive crew, outstanding meal service and comfortable seating, I always feel as though I am flying first class. I am now a frequent flyer and very happy customer. I now hope to join your team in providing this fantastic service."

Do you think we have a good reputation?

"Absolutely! Through my own experience, I have encountered attentive and efficient crew, fantastic meals and comfortable seating. In researching the airline, it appears that others agree with these observations.

The variety of awards the airline has received over the years is a sure testament to its fantastic reputation."

What is the worst thing you have heard about us?

"The worst thing I have heard about Emirates is that competition for jobs is fierce because it is such a terrific airline. Everything else I have heard, have been overly positive."

Is there anything you think we do badly?

"In conducting my research into the airline, I haven't come across anything to suggest that you are doing anything badly. In fact, I have discovered quite the opposite.

Plus, I am sure you wouldn't enjoy your current success and be receiving so many awards for excellence if you were doing anything really wrong."

How do you feel about working for a large airline?

"I welcome the opportunity to work in a large, developed and well known airline such as Emirates. The resources and potential for advancement are not available in smaller airlines. I'd be proud to apply my skills and abilities to the excellence that flourishes here."

ASCERTAINING YOUR
SUITABILITY

Tell me

ABOUT YOURSELF

While this question is often used to break the ice, it is also asked to gain a true sense of who you are. Its open-ended and unstructured approach will reveal a great deal about you and what you feel is important.

The best approach is to provide a short paraphrased overview of what you do, why you are attending the interview and what you have to offer.

"As you can see from my résumé, I currently work as a freelance hair consultant, and have worked in client-facing roles for the past eight years. During this time, I have worked my way up from a receptionist to a senior hair stylist, while simultaneously studying for my NVQ levels 1, 2 and 3.

Now, this brings me to why I am here today, interviewing with you.

I have always wanted to become cabin crew and, during the course of my career, I have been gradually mastering the skills needed to perform its tasks. I'm confident that the customer care and teamwork skills I have developed throughout the course of my career, combined with my friendly and positive nature, will complement your existing team and enable me to deliver the standard of service that passengers have come to expect from Emirates.

I'd now like to discuss how I might contribute to the success of Emriates by joining your team."

Why should

WE HIRE YOU?

This is the time to shine, so don't be modest. Consider the experience and character traits that are most relevant and transferable to the position and explain how you have demonstrated these in the past.

Try it with the A.B.C formula...

A: Answer
"Because I am a good fit for the position and Emirates' corporate culture."

B: Back it up
"As you can see from my résumé I have worked in client facing roles for the past eight years, so I am certainly qualified to perform the diverse requirements of this role. Also, the fact that I have been promoted through the ranks is a clear testament to my abilities and the confidence my manager had in me. More significantly, however, my character is tailored to the role. As you will have observed during the group assessments, I am a very welcoming and social individual who interacts well with others. I readily adapt to new people and environments, I am hard working and think fast on my feet."

C: Conclude
"I am confident that these aspects of my personality and experience will enable me to perform the job to the same high standard that exists currently and I believe I would be a valuable asset to Emirates."

What are

YOUR BEST QUALITIES?

With this question, you need to read between the lines. The interviewer is not interested in your best qualities per se, but what qualities you have that would make you a good fit for the position. So tailor your answer to the requirements of the job and be sure to back it up with examples.

Try it with the A.B.C formula...

A: Answer
"As you will have observed during the group assessments, I am a very welcoming and social individual who interacts well with others, and readily adapts to new people and environments."

B: Back it up
"In fact, my previous supervisor also picked up on these attributes and often asked me to carry out the shampoo because she knew I would make the clients feel welcome and relaxed"

C: Conclude
"I am confident that these aspects of my character will enable me to perform the job to the same high standard that exists currently within Emirates"

What is

YOUR GREATEST WEAKNESS?

The key to answering questions about weaknesses is to focus your response on those skills you are actively learning or planning to develop. This could be assertiveness or leadership. The point is, it is only a weakness because you haven't yet mastered it, and that is why you are working on developing those skills further. Be mindful, however, to not reveal weaknesses that are a major requirement fo the job.

Try it with the A.C.T formula...

A: Attack
"I recognise that my leadership ability is a potential area of improvement"

C: Clarify
"Which is why I am actively working on developing this area further through a part time training course at my local college"

T: Turn
"Although I am still learning, I see constant improvement in my capabilities when being faced with leadership tasks and I am confident that I will continue to learn and grow with experience"

Are you an introvert or extrovert?

"Actually, I would describe myself as an ambivert because I enjoy social interaction, but am equally happy to spend time alone in my own company."

What makes you stand out from the crowd?

"My friendly and positive nature certainly defines me as a person and makes me stand out from the crowd. I adopt a very optimistic view in every aspect of my life and refuse to allow external circumstances to negatively affect my state."

If you had to characterise yourself in one sentence, what would you say?

"I am a friendly and approachable person, who is sincere and very optimistic about life."

Rate yourself on a scale from 1 to 10

"I would rate myself as an 8. I always give my best, but in doing so I increase my skills. I, therefore, always see room for improvement."

How would a friend describe you?

"My friends would describe me as sociable, cheerful and optimistic. They would also say I am someone who thinks fast on my feet and stays calm in adverse situations."

How would an enemy describe your character?

"I suppose they might say that I am tenacious because I don't give in without a struggle, but am realistic about my limits. They might say I am brave because I am prepared to confront issues when there is a need, but I weigh the consequences and don't act irresponsibly. And, maybe, driven because I push for what I want, but can back off when advisable to do so."

How have you changed in the last five years?

"I feel like I have matured rather than aged five years. The skills I have acquired and the qualities I have developed have changed me enormously, and I know there are parts of me that are still not being utilised half as effectively as they could be. My customer care and communication skills have definitely been improved, and I have a better ability to use my initiative and think on my feet."

What is the importance of having good communication skills?

"The ability to speak clearly, listen actively and comprehend effectively is vital for our successful interaction with others, and continued growth."

How confident are you about addressing a group?

"I used to be nervous about speaking in front of a group, yet I found that preparation, practice and knowing my subject helped me overcome this, I still experience the occasional butterflies, as anyone who cares about doing a good job does, but I now understand how to effectively ground myself and have no problems addressing a group."

How would you define good customer service?

"Good customer service is about constantly and consistently meeting customer's expectations by providing a friendly, efficient and reliable service throughout the life of the service and/or product.

Excellent customer service is about exceeding customer's expectations by going beyond the call of duty. I believe that because no two customers are the same, they deserve to receive a service that is tailored to their individual needs. This is where a service moves beyond being just a satisfactory one, and becomes an excellent one."

What do you think constitutes poor customer service?

"Poor service is when customers are treated with disrespect and provided with a poor quality product and/or service by rude, ignorant and unhelpful staff."

Do you think the customer is always right?

"Whilst every customer is important, they are certainly not always right. Those who exhibit abusive behaviour, or do anything to compromise safety are straying beyond the boundary."

When have you witnessed good customer service?

"I remember when I visited a local restaurant for a luncheon. It had just turned 3pm on a Wednesday afternoon and, much to mine and the management's surprise, they were exceptionally busy with only three waiting staff on duty. Despite the overwhelming rush our waitress, Claire, was very polite and helpful. The staff showed great teamwork as they managed to pull together and deliver an outstanding service."

When have you witnessed poor customer service?

"I needed a particular material for a dress I was making. In most stores the salesperson would give me a quick 'no' before I finished explaining what I was looking for. I hadn't really noticed until I experienced the opposite service in another smaller fabric store."

What do you enjoy about providing customer care?

"The most enjoyable aspect I would have to say is that because I genuinely care about my client's satisfaction, it rewards me personally when I know that they are happy with the job I did. This, in turn, drives me to do better."

What do you dislike about providing customer care?

"Providing good customer care can be a challenge, and some people may view that negatively, but I view each challenge as an opportunity to develop and grow. So, because I am committed to developing myself, I welcome and enjoy the challenges of providing customer care. It is something I have become very good at."

What do you find most challenging about providing customer service?

"Providing customer service is a challenge in itself. Because people are unpredictable by their very nature, you have to always expect the unexpected and be prepared to go beyond the call of duty and deal with issues as they arrive."

How would you define teamwork?

"Teamwork is a group of people who work cooperatively together to achieve a common goal. They make a coordinated effort and each individual contributes their unique skills and ideas to the task."

Do you prefer to work alone or as part of a team?

"I am happy either way, and equally efficient at both. So, whether I prefer to work alone or in a team would depend on the best way to complete the job.

I do, however, have a preference towards team spirit. As well as the interaction, there is greater satisfaction when you share the joy of completing a task."

Are you a team player?

"Absolutely I am. As you will have observed during the group assessments, I interact well with others, and readily adapt to new people. I am a good listener, I respect other people's opinions and I can be relied on to contribute to the overall goal.

In fact, my previous supervisor used to say that my infectious optimism created excitement in other team members and resulted in a greater team effort and higher output."

What role do you assume in a team situation?

"I am whatever I need to be. If a situation comes up and someone needs to take charge, then I will. But if someone else has already taken charge and is solving it, I will follow their lead."

What do you enjoy about working as part of a team?

"There's nothing like being part of a great team where you can learn from the other members, bounce ideas off one another, and share achievements and rewards. There is a unique feeling of camaraderie that can never be experienced from working alone."

What do you least enjoy about working as part of a team?

"People not pulling their weight can be frustrating. However, I've noticed that such people simply lack enthusiasm or confidence, and that energetic and cheerful coworkers can often change that."

What do you find most challenging about being part of a team?

"The most challenging aspect is inspiring and motivating other team members. Each has different needs and is motivated by different things."

Are you happy to be supervised by people who are younger than yourself?

"Absolutely. I don't consider age to be an important factor. What matters is a person's credibility, professionalism and competency."

Why did you

LEAVE YOUR LAST JOB?

While you do need to be honest about your reasons for leaving past employment, you need to be diplomatic in your response. Being bored or not getting along with your boss are not ideal answers here. Be positive and be concise.

No opportunities
"While I enjoyed working for my previous employer, and appreciate the skills I developed while I was there, I felt I was not being challenged enough in the job. After working my way up through the company, there were no further opportunities for advancement."

Redundancy
"I survived the first layoffs, but unfortunately this one got me."

Note: Be prepared to be asked how many people were laid off.

Temporary post
"The job was only a temporary position, which I took to broaden my experience."

How to deal

WITH BEING FIRED

If you have a termination on your record, the recruiters will not care if the termination was unjust, unfair or has a good explanation, a termination is a big red flag, so you need to do everything you can to avoid disclosing it.

In the first instance, you may choose to omit the information. Omitting details is not the same as telling an outright lie or making a false statement. When asked for reference details, simply choose another referee.

If you have just been fired from your most recent employment, they will not know unless you tell them. So you could mark your employment to present and leave it at that. If asked if they can call your employer for a reference, it would not raise any eyebrows if you respectfully decline due to your ongoing employment.

The third option is to take proactive measures to have the termination designation changed.

If the termination occurred some time ago, it is more likely that the employer will be open to changing the designation if you accept responsibility and demonstrate a sincere regret for the situation. Simply advise them that the termination is damaging your chances of gaining employment and you would like the designation changed to something neutral, such as laid off or resigned.

If you would feel uncomfortable or unethical to omit such a detail and would prefer to take accountability for what happened, be sure to downplay the termination on your application form by simply stating 'will explain at interview'. You will have some damage control to contend with, so remember to accept the mistake, don't blame others and don't make any excuses. Stick to the facts, point out what went wrong and what you have learned from the experience.

Whichever route you take, there is a risk. Either you not be hired by admitting to the termination or you may not be hired because you did not disclose it and were caught out. The decision has to be yours.

Why were you
FIRED?

If you choose to reveal your termination, be sure to accept the mistake, don't make excuses or blame others. Stick to the facts, point out what went wrong and what you have learnt from the experience.

Incompatibility

"I was desperate for work and took the job without fully understanding the expectations. It turned out that my competencies were not a right match for the employer's needs, so we agreed that it was time for me to move on to a position that would be more suitable. I certainly learnt a great deal from this experience and it's not a mistake I will ever repeat."

Personal reasons

"I had been going through a rough patch in my personal life which, unfortunately, upset my work life. It is regrettable and my circumstances have now changed, but I really wasn't in the position to avoid it at the time."

Immaturity

"I was a recent college graduate and didn't have the maturity and respect for work or a career that I now have. I have certainly grown up a lot since then, and I now understand what it is I want to do with my life."

Never:

» Badmouth previous employers, colleagues or bosses.

» Place blame

» Tell lies

» Reveal team incompatibility

Why have you
HAD SO MANY JOBS?

A fragmented work history will give the impression of a job hopper and will raise serious doubts about your commitment.

Whatever the reason, whether you have held temporary agency contracts, have been struggling to find something that you can feel committed to, or have simply been trying to gain a more rounded skill-set, it is important to put a positive spin on it, so that you can avoid any negative and rash assumptions being made.

Broaden experience
"I wanted to experience different jobs to broaden my knowledge, skills and experience. This has provided me with a very valuable and rounded skill set."

Temporary positions
"Due to the lack of full time opportunities in my area, I was only able to secure short term contracts."

Youth
In my youth, I was unsure about the direction I wanted to take in my career. I have matured a great deal since those days and am now interested in establishing myself into a long term opportunity.

What do you dislike

ABOUT YOUR CURRENT JOB?

There will always be less than exciting aspects of a job, however, being critical about your job isn't going to create a positive impression. So, soften these aspects as much as possible and try to select neutral examples, such as paperwork, lack of job security or opportunities for growth.

"I honestly can't think of any major dislikes. I don't think I'd be able to really excel if I weren't truly interested in the work, or if I were merely motivated by its financial rewards. I guess my answer will have to come under the category or nuisances.

The biggest nuisance is the paperwork. I realise the importance of documentation, and I cooperatively fill out the forms, but I'm always looking for efficiencies in that area that will get me out in front of the client where I belong."

Why were you
UNEMPLOYED FOR SO LONG?

It is better to say that you chose to take time off between jobs than it is to give the impression that you were unemployable.

Study
"I wanted to broaden my knowledge base, so I went back into full time study."

Travel
"I wanted to experience the world before settling into a long term career. I am now ready to commit."

Youth
"In my youth, I felt confused about the direction I wanted my career to take. I am now much more mature and certain in my desired direction."

Personal reasons
"Personal circumstances prohibited me from taking gainful employment, however, circumstances have now changed and I am ready to get back to work."

Why did you stay with the same employer for so long?

"I was there for several years, but in a variety of different roles. The opportunities for growth were fantastic so it felt as though I was undergoing frequent changes without actually changing employer. I didn't see the need to move on."

Why have you decided to change professions at this stage of your career?

"This career turnaround hasn't come suddenly. I have always wanted to become cabin crew and have been gradually mastering the skills needed to perform its tasks. I have now reached a point in my life where I am prepared to make the career and lifestyle change. I want to take advantage of that opportunity while it is presented to me."

What do you like about your current job?

"Rather than pick out the little details of the routine work, here are three general things. First is customer satisfaction. Seeing a client's face glow with happiness when their hair is transformed gives me an intense feeling of pride. Second is the interaction I get with my colleagues and clients. Finally, I enjoy being creative and finding new ways to please the customer."

Which particular aspect of your work do you find most frustrating?

"That's an interesting question because I am, generally speaking, a tolerant person. Slow periods can be sources of frustration, but at times like that I put more effort into advertising and establishing new clientele. That way, the slow periods don't last long."

What contribution can you make to ensure passengers will fly with us again?

My customer service experience and friendly character style will enable me to deliver a superior standard of service which will make passengers feel welcome, valued and relaxed.

Why should we hire you instead of someone with cabin crew experience?

"Although I might not have cabin crew experience, I have the necessary skills to make an impressive start, and the willingness to learn and improve. Sometimes, employers do better when they hire people who don't have a great deal of repetitive experience. That way, they can train these employees in their methods and ways of doing the job. Training is much easier than untraining."

Why should we hire you for this position rather than another applicant?

"I can't tell you why you should hire me instead of another candidate but, I can tell you why you should hire me."

Are you willing to start as a trainee?

"Yes, absolutely. This is a new area for me, and I believe in getting a good foundation in the basics before progressing. An entry level position will enable me to learn the position inside out, and will give me the opportunity to grow when I prove myself. I also have a great deal of knowledge and work experience, which I'm sure will contribute to my successful progression through training."

How do you feel about the probationary period?

"I can see no problem with a probationary period. I am a fast learner so it shouldn't take me long to prove myself."

How do you feel about working at Christmas, and other special occasions?

"Naturally, I would miss spending time with my friends and family, but my career is important to me and my family and friends respect and appreciate that fact. I am happy to make the sacrifice as necessary."

How do you feel about a formal dress code?

"I have always liked to dress formally and feel very comfortable wearing formal attire. I realise that a standard of dress is necessary in order to project a professional image to the passengers."

This is a long hours culture, is that a problem for you?

"I understand that this a demanding job, but I really do thrive on the challenge of this sort of work and have worked long hours in the past, so I am willing to work whatever hours are necessary to get the work done."

This position will involve relocating, how will you adjust to the different lifestyle?

"I realise that this position involves transfers, and I bore that in mind when I applied. I am fully aware of what to expect from the research I have done and would welcome the different lifestyle."

How do you feel about the routine tasks and irregular hours of this job?

"I accept that every role carries with it a certain amount of routine in order to get the job done. If my job involves repetitive work, it is my responsibility to carry it out to the best of my abilities. As for irregular hours I would expect to have an indication of my core hours, but will work the hours that are necessary in order to fulfil the requirements of the role."

Do you feel confident in your ability to handle this position?

"Yes, absolutely. I'm very confident in my abilities. I'm familiar with the basic job requirements and I learn quickly. It undoubtedly will take time and effort on my part, but I'm more than willing to devote that time and effort."

Do you feel ready for a more responsible position?

"Absolutely. I believe that eight years experience working closely with customers, has prepared me professionally and personally to move up to this role. My customer care and teamwork skills have been finely tuned over the years, and I know I am capable of greater achievements."

How will you cope with the change in environment?

"I welcome the challenge of learning about and adapting to a new environment, that's one of the reasons I'm seeking to make a career change right now. Any major change, while always containing some challenge is a chance to grow, learn, and advance."

Do you work well under pressure?

"Absolutely. Because pressure is the result of a new challenge, I perceive pressure as an opportunity to develop and grow. The more challenges I experience, the better my skills become, and the less I feel the pressure of subsequent challenges. So, because I am committed to developing myself, I welcome the challenges of pressure."

How would I know you were under pressure?

"I disguise my pressure well, therefore, I would hope that it wouldn't be obvious enough to notice."

What types of people annoy you or try your patience?

"That's an interesting question, because I am a very tolerant person. However, there are instances where my patience is put to the test, but I am able to control myself and my emotions, so I never let my patience move beyond the testing stage."

Do you have difficulties tolerating people with different views than you?

"No. I recognise that everyone has their own views, and that they may not always correspond with my own. Differing views and personalities are what make us individual, so I don't let other people's views or interests affect how I feel about them."

How often do you lose your temper?

"I never lose my temper. I regard that sort of behaviour as counterproductive and inappropriate. By losing your temper, you cannot possibly resolve a problem. Even if you're completely right, losing your temper often destroys your ability to convince others of this."

What makes you angry or impatient?

"Anger to me means loss of control, and I'm not the kind of person who loses control. It is counterproductive and inappropriate, and doesn't gain anything of value.

When I feel stress building up, instead of getting angry or impatient, I take a deep breath and begin to focus on the positives. The results are quite dramatic, my whole demeanour changes very rapidly,"

How do you handle criticism?

"As long as the criticism is fair and constructive, I listen to it and remain gracious. I thank them for their candid feedback, express regret over the situation and modify my future behaviour accordingly."

DETERMINING YOUR
COMPETENCIES

1 When have you gone out of your way for a customer?

Sample Response 1

Situation:
I had a client call into the store who was looking for a very specific style of fabric. She had visited several stores in and around the area but hadn't been successful in her search.

I could see that she was exhausted, but also very determined. She spoke with such sorrow in her voice that I actually began to feel sorry for the poor lady because I didn't have the fabric to sell her.

Action:
Not wanting to be the bearer of more bad news, I decided to offer my assistance. I spent several hours ringing around wholesalers, distributors and manufacturers trying to track down this particular fabric, when finally I struck gold with a small manufacturing plant.

Result:
Because the fabric was a special order, there was a small handling charge, but the customer received the fabric within a few days and was sure it was worth the expense and wait.

Sample Response 2

Situation:
I encountered a problem when one of my clients was unable to have a hair treatment carried out in her home because it was being renovated.

Action:
In an attempt to keep the client, I spoke to a contact I had within a local salon and was able to negotiate a small fee for use of the salon facilities.

Result:
This worked out really well because it was convenient for both myself and the client to travel to. Since then, I have negotiated similar deals with four other salons and have increased my customer base dramatically as a direct result.

2 Describe a time when your customer service could have been better?

Evaluation

Providing excellent customer service is vital, so you should be very cautious when providing negative examples.

You could take a modest approach and explain that you always strive to do better, or you could be honest with humble example.

Alternatively, you could attempt to avoid providing an example by explaining how you maintain your standards, and then proceed with an example of a time when you have demonstrated this capability.

Sample Response (Modest approach)

I take great pride in providing the best service I possibly can, but in doing so I increase my skills and can always see room for improvement.

Sample Response (No experience)

I take great pride in providing the best service I possibly can, and I never let my standards slip. Even during times of high pressure, I make an effort to remain courteous and helpful. I can honestly say that I have never received any negative feedback.

When have you solved a customer problem?

Sample Response

Situation:
I remember a client who came to me to have her hair extensions replaced. She had worn sewn in extensions for several months and was experiencing some discomfort from the attachments.

Action:
As I examined her hair, I was shocked to discover how much damage had been caused. Her roots had become severely matted and the tightness from the installed tracks had created spots of baldness.

I took a moment to analyse the situation, work out a strategy and then I set to work.

I spent several hours meticulously untangling every hair and removing every extension piece, The more I removed, the more I could see the scale of the damage that had been caused. Sadly, the client's hair was in very bad shape after the removal and the spots of baldness were very evident. Needless to say, I had a very emotional customer.

I applied a very deep conditioning protein treatment to the customers remaining locks and gave it a good trim. I then finished up with some fine and strategically placed fusion hair extensions to conceal the bald patches and create some much needed volume.

Result:
Following the treatment, the client looked fantastic and her smile was restored. Her hair soon returned to its former glory and she became a regular client of mine.

When have you tended to an upset customer?

Sample Response

Situation:
I recently experienced a situation with a client who was having relationship problems. She was becoming increasingly emotional and I could sense that she was feeling very depressed.

Action:
Although I felt compassion for her situation, I knew that it was important for me not to get overly involved. So, I gave her chance to talk while I listened, and I tried to show empathy while remaining neutral and professional in my response.

Result:
Just being able to talk to someone who listened seemed to make her feel better. As she continued to speak, she appeared to have gained a deeper insight into her situation and actually began seeing things more positively. Consequently, she was able to calmly discuss her feelings with her partner and work through their problems. She later thanked me for listening.

Reflection:
From this experience, I learned that just listening can be providing good customer care.

5 Have you been confronted by an aggressive customer?

Evaluation

The ability to remain well-mannered and well-tempered while dealing with an aggressive customer is an absolute necessity. The recruiter will want to assess whether you can deal with confrontational issues in a calm and rational manner.

You will be assessed on how well you coped under the pressure and how you dealt with the customer. A good response will show that you never lost your temper and remained courteous throughout the experience.

Sample Response

Situation:
Shortly after I began freelancing, I encountered a problem when an associate of mine tried to pressure me into a free service based on friendship.

Action:
I proceeded to offer her, what I considered to be, a reasonable discount, but she was not satisfied with my offer and proceeded to pressure me with emotional blackmail. I remained cordial, but became more assertive as I continued to refuse her demands.

Result:
Rather than accept the reasons for my decision, she became increasingly enraged, and even began to slander my service and friendship

Shocked at her over-reaction, and concerned about what might develop, I felt I had no option but to withdraw from the situation.

Reflection:
This experience was very challenging and certainly tested my patience. But I remained calm and, although this particular relationship never recovered, it was a learning experience that hasn't since been repeated.

6   When have you had to say 'No' to a customer?

Sample Response

Situation:
I remember when a customer tried to return a pair of trainers to the store for a refund. Although the customer denied it, I could see that the shoes had clearly been worn.

Action:
I remained calm and polite as I suggested that the shoes could not be returned unless faulty or unused.

The customer become very aggressive and repeatedly threatened to contact our head office to complain about me if I didn't refund him immediately.

I remained assertive and suggested this would be the best course of action for him to take. I then proceeded to provide him with the full details of our complaints manager within the head office.

Result:
Realising defeat, the man stormed out of the shop and, to my knowledge, never did take the matter further.

7 When have you handled a customer complaint?

Evaluation

The recruiter wants to know that you are able to retain your composure and use your problem solving skills when dealing with a dissatisfied customer.

A good response will show that you never took the complaint personally, remained calm and courteous, and were able to create a satisfactory outcome for the customer.

Sample Response

Situation:
I remember when a customer complained about a meal they had purchased.

Because over two thirds of the entire course had been eaten, not only was it obvious that the complaint was insincere, but it was also against the restaurants policy to offer a refund under such circumstances.

The customer was becoming very enraged and threatened to write to the trading standards and newspapers if I did not give him a full refund.

Action:
I gave the customer my undivided attention while he vented his frustrations. Then, when he had finally calmed down, I calmly apologised for the dissatisfaction and proceeded to offer a meal deal voucher as a goodwill gesture.

Result:
The customer was clearly unhappy not to have received a refund, but he left the restaurant and, as suspected, never did take the matter any further.

8   When have you had to resolve a conflict between what the customer wanted and what you could realistically deliver?

Sample Response

Situation:
I remember a client who came to me for a colour treatment and restyle. She had used a virtual hairstyle software to create her ideal look and was beaming with excitement as she showed me the picture.

The style was notably very pretty, and it was clear that it was ideally suited to the client. Unfortunately, however, the client's hair had been through several perming and colour treatments, and the platinum blonde shade that she wanted just wasn't going to be possible at that time.

Action:
Knowing how excited the client was, I felt a little dejected as I proceeded to break this news to her. In the hope of relieving some of her obvious disappointment, I suggested a strand test to see if it would be possible to lift some of the colour without causing excessive damage. If the strand test were a success, we could perform a gradual transformation through the use of highlights.

Result:
Thankfully, the strand test was a success and the client, while naturally disappointed, was happy to go ahead with the gradual transformation. The result was striking, and the client was happy with the result.

Within nine months, the transformation was complete, and I had a very satisfied customer.

9 Describe a situation when the customer was wrong

Evaluation

Although the popular saying suggests otherwise, the customer isn't always right and the recruiter wants to know that you aren't Intimidated by such situations.

You will be assessed on how you approached the customer and went about dealing the situation. A good response will demonstrate your ability to use tact, and will show that you remained courteous throughout the experience.

Sample Response

Situation:
I remember a client who I had carried out a perming treatment for. After completing the treatment, I provided written instructions for how to care for her new perm which specifically instructed against washing the hair for at least 48 hours.

Unfortunately, the very next day the client washed her hair and the perm dropped out. The client was understandably very upset, but refused to accept that the perm had fallen out as a consequence of her own actions. She became very irate and started to slander my work and the salon.

Action:
When asked if she had followed the instructions, she denied being provided with any. I assured her that instructions were provided, and suggested she check her belongings.

Result:
Later that afternoon, the client returned to the salon holding onto the instruction sheet with a very embarrassed look on her face. She apologised profusely for her behaviour.

Reflection:
To avoid a repeat of this situation, I now provide clearer warnings within the written information sheet and back it up with verbal instructions.

10 Have you ever bent the rules for a customer?

Evaluation

There are situations where it is permissible to bend the rules, however, some airlines may view rule bending very negatively. So, no matter how trivial or well-intended, you may want to play it safe and declare that you have never gone against the rules.

If you do decide to provide an answer, you should show that you are able to keep balance between company policy and the interest of customers.

Sample Response

I have always abided by company policies and have never bent the rules. Bending the rules for one customer, will no doubt lead to a downward spiral . Either the customer will expect further rule bending, or other customers will catch on and expect the same treatment. It's just not a wise course of action to take.

11 Tell me about a time when you failed to communicate effectively?

Evaluation

We all experience challenges in communication, but a complete failure to communicate effectively will show a lack of initiative and creativity in problem solving.

Whatever the reason for a communication challenge, there is always a way to communicate if you are willing to put in some additional effort. Your answer should reflect this.

Sample Response (Modest Approach)

While I have certainly encountered communication challenges, I can honestly say that I have never yet completely failed in my ability to communicate. With some creativity, I have always found a way to overcome communication barriers.

Sample Response (Humble Example)

Situation:
Generally, I am a very efficient communicator, but I do recall when I experienced difficulty communicating with an OAP client.

Action:
The client was very hard of hearing, and I tried everything to communicate with her. I spoke slower, louder, used hand gestures and facial expressions, I even tried to write the information down, but without her glasses she was unable see my writing clearly.

Result:
Fortunately, I managed to locate a magnifying glass, which enabled the client to read my instructions, and everything worked out well in the end.

12 When have your communication skills made a difference to a situation or outcome?

Evaluation

The ability to communicate well is vital to the role of cabin crew, so you should have plenty of real life examples ready to share. This is your chance to shine, so don't be modest.

Sample Response

Situation:
I remember a trainee apprentice we had in our department who never asked questions and refused all offers of help. Unfortunately, instead of trying to understand her reasons, everyone drew the conclusion that she was a know-it-all and vowed not to offer help in the future.

Action:
Concerned that her progress would suffer, I decided to offer my encouragement and support. It soon became evident from our conversation that she had excessively high expectations of herself and feared looking incompetent. I explained that it was okay to ask questions, and mistakes were expected. I even shared a few of my own early mishaps to lighten the mood.

Result:
Very quickly after that we saw a change in her behaviour. She began asking questions, she was more open to suggestions, and her skills improved immensely.

Reflection:
From this experience, I learnt that things are not always what they appear and we need to be more objective before making rash judgements.

13

Give an example of when you had to present complex information in a simplified manner in order to explain it to others

Sample Response

Situation:
I remember a client who was interested in having a colour treatment carried out. She was very inquisitive and asked numerous questions, so I could sense that she was concerned about the process and potential damage to her natural hair.

Action:
Not satisfied with a simple nontechnical version, I had to provide a detailed technical breakdown of the whole process. This involved describing the molecular structure of the hair, the effect colour particles have and how they bond to the structure.

Result:
Although I had to occasionally refer to training manuals to emphasise or clarify my point, overall the client was satisfied with my effort. As a direct result, she went ahead with the treatment and was very pleased with the outcome.

14 Have you ever had to overcome a language barrier?

Evaluation

As cabin crew, you will interact with a variety of people from a broad range of cultures and backgrounds. The ability to relate to others and adapt your communication style is, therefore, very important.

Sample Response

Situation:
During a trip to Africa, I became acquainted with a French lady. She understood my French, the little amount I knew, but she didn't really understand English. Unfortunately, the amount of French I knew wasn't enough to get me through a whole conversation, so I had to improvise.

Action:
I spoke French wherever possible and filled in the gaps with improvised sign language and facial expressions.

Result:
At first it was a little tricky trying to find imaginative ways to communicate, but over time I became much more proficient. I'm sure she was amused by my amateur efforts, but it worked out well and I came away with a new friend.

Reflection:
Now when I encounter this type of communication barrier, I am much more confident in my ability to cope.

15 Tell me about a time that you had to work as part of a team

Evaluation

The ability to work well within a team is absolutely essential to working as cabin crew. You should, therefore, have plenty of examples that demonstrate this ability.

Sample Response

Situation:
There was a particular time that stands out for me because it was such an unusual occurrence.

It was a usual quiet Tuesday afternoon and only myself, the senior stylist, an apprentice, and the salon manager were on duty. To our surprise, it was as if someone started offering out free chocolate, as clients started to filter through the doors.

Action:
Despite the overwhelming rush, we showed great teamwork as we pulled together and shared our duties. Even our manager showed great team spirit as she got involved with the hair service.

Result:
As a result of our teamwork, and some free relaxing conditioning treatments, we managed to deliver an outstanding service. Every client went away completely satisfied.

16   When have you struggled to fit in?

Evaluation

With the constant rotation of crew, there will be some people that you don't immediately hit it off with. The recruiters want to know that you aren't intimidated by such difficulties and are able to move past any struggles.

Sample Response

Situation:

When I started working at Trina's Hair & Beauty, I was joining a very close-knit team who had been together for a number of years.

As a result of the number of trainees they had witnessed come and go over the years, they had become a little reluctant to accept new trainees.

I wouldn't say it was a struggle to fit in as such, but I certainly experienced some growing pains. With remarks such as 'if you are still here then' to contend with, I knew I had to prove myself.

Action:

To show that I was serious about the job, and was not a fly-by-night, I focused a lot of effort on learning my new job. At the same time, I continued to be friendly and respectful of my new colleagues while I made a conscious effort to get to know them.

Result:

As a result of my hard effort, It didn't take long for them to accept me and include me as part of their team. Naturally, I have become closer to some of my colleagues than with others, but we all got on and worked well as a team.

17 Have you ever experienced difficulties getting along with colleagues?

Evaluation

No matter how hard we try, or how likeable we are, there will always be someone that we don't hit it off with. To say otherwise, would not sound credible.

For the most part, this question is asked to determine your ability to get along with other people and manage adversity. The recruiters want to know that you don't allow conflict to interfere with work.

The best answer should show that you aren't intimidated or confrontational in such situations, but you put in the commitment necessary to build a respectful and healthy working relationship.

Sample Response

Situation:
I remember one co-worker in particular who flat out didn't like me. It didn't matter what I did or said, or whether I tried to avoid or befriend this person.

Action:
After a couple of days of subtle hostility, I decided to assert myself. I diplomatically explained that I acknowledged her dislike for me and I asked for input as to what I must do to create a professional relationship

Result:
Although we never became friends, we were able to maintain more cordial relations thereafter.

18 Tell us about a challenge you have faced with a colleague

Evaluation

Airlines have a constant rotation of crew on-board each aircraft and, especially within larger airlines, you may not work with the same crew members twice. As a result, it is guaranteed that you will encounter challenging situations with colleagues.

The recruiters want to know that you aren't intimidated by such colleagues or situations, and are prepared to use your initiative to diffuse or mediate as necessary to keep working relationships healthy.

Your answer should demonstrate your willingness to cooperate with others to resolve differences, improve relations, and manage conflicts. It should also display your ability to remain patient and positive in the face of adversity.

Sample Response

Situation:
I do remember one situation where two of my colleagues really didn't hit it off with one another. They were constantly quarrelling and everyone had lost patience with them, but no one wanted to get involved.

Action:
In the end, I decided to take the initiative and act as a sort of mediator to the situation. I was not their manager, so I had to be as tactful as I could so that I wouldn't upset anyone.

I started by explaining that I acknowledged their dislike for each other and then I drew upon the fact that they are both professionals and can, therefore, put aside their differences for the good of the team.

Result:
They had a pretty frank discussion and, although I can't say they ended up the best of friends, they did work out an effective strategy for working more productively together.

19 Tell me about a disagreement with a colleague

Sample Response

Introduction:
Working in a creative environment with other highly skilled professionals, it was natural that we had the occassional clash of ideas. Any disagreements we did have, however, were so relatively minor and insignificant that I would be hard pressed to recall the exact details.

Situation:
Our disagreements were usually as a result of our individual preference towards certain products, styles, magazines or equipment.

Action:
Our debates were never confrontational and they never interfered with our work in any way.

Result:
In fact, some very interesting views emerged from these debates which sometimes resulted in people, including myself, having a slight change in my perspective. So, they were often very educational.

20 Have you successfully worked with a difficult coworker?

Evaluation

The recruiters want to know that you aren't intimidated by difficult colleagues or situations, and are prepared to use your initiative to deal with the situation as necessary. You will be assessed on how you approached the colleague and how you dealt with the situation.

Your answer should demonstrate your willingness to co-operate with others to resolve differences, improve relations, and manage conflicts. It should also display your ability to remain patient and positive when challenging situations occur.

Sample Response

Situation:
I remember one member of staff was always complaining. Nothing was ever good enough or couldn't possibly work. Everyone had lost patience with her but, because she was so incredibly sensitive, no one said anything.

Action:
I spent some time with her and tactfully told her that it appeared as if she was always putting our ideas down.

Result:
On hearing this feedback she was genuinely horrified at her own behaviour. She explained that she hadn't realised it had made everyone feel that way and agreed that from then on she would try to be more positive.

Very quickly after that we saw a change in her behaviour. She became more conscious of her own attitude and deliberately tried to be more considerate. From that point on, no one could have hoped for a more committed team member.

21 Have you ever worked with someone you disliked?

Sample Response

Situation:
There was one colleague I worked with that I really found it difficult to get along with personally.

Action:
Instead of focusing on those things I didn't like, I put my personal views aside and focused on the skills she brought to the position.

Result:
My personal view of her never changed, and we never became friends, but we did work productively alongside each other without any problems.

22 Have you ever acted as a mentor to a coworker?

Evaluation

There may be times when you have to mentor new crew members and the recruiters are trying to assess your ability to lead and mentor your colleagues.

Sample Response

Situation:
I remember when one of our trainees was having problems understanding certain aspects of her course material, and I could see she was becoming increasingly frustrated and self critical.

Action:
Having witnessed her in action, I knew that she was a very bright and talented individual with no obvious lack of skill. So, I determined that her frustrations were probably the result of the pressure she was feeling about her approaching exam.

Concerned at the effect this pressure was having on her, and having experienced the same pressures myself, I decided to offer my support. To reinforce her understanding, I demonstrated some of the techniques she had been struggling with and showed her a few memory tips and tricks which had helped me through my exams.

Result:
My breakdown of the processes, along with the visual demonstration I provided, seemed to make the material much more understandable for her. In the days that followed, she seemed to have a new lease of life and was much more positive. Subsequently, she passed her exams with top grades.

23 What have you done that shows initiative?

Evaluation

Your answer here should show that you take the initiative when it comes to additional work and demonstrate a natural desire for doing extra tasks willingly.

Sample Response

Situation:
When I began working for my current employer, the inventory system was outdated and the storage room was very messy and disorganised.

Action:
I came in on my day off, cleaned up the mess, organised the store cupboards and catalogued it all on the new inventory forms.

Result:
Thereafter, when orders arrived it was easy to organise and retrieve.

Reflection:
If I'm able to do the task, instead of waiting for the job to be done, I simply do it.

24 Have you undertaken a course of study, on your own initiative, in order to improve your work performance?

Evaluation

Your answer here should show that you are committed to self-development and take the initiative when it comes to improving yourself and your efficiency.

Sample Response

Situation:
While at Trina's Hair Salon, we were experiencing a spectacular rise in demand for high fashion cuts. I had some creative cutting experience, but nothing that extended to the kind of advanced skill that was required for true high fashion cuts.

Action:
After some consideration, I decided that increasing my creative cutting skills would not only give the salon a competitive advantage, but it would also be a fantastic opportunity for me to move my skills to the next level. So, I took the initiative and, under my own funding, immediately enrolled onto a creative cutting course.

Result:
My new skills proved to be an instant success. Existing clients began recommending me to their friends, which resulted in a massive rise in clientele. Needless to say, my manager was very happy.

25 Describe an improvement that you personally initiated

Evaluation

The recruiter wants to know that you seek better and more effective ways of carrying out your work and can suggest improvements that will achieve more efficiency.

Your answer here should show that you take the initiative when it comes to improving working methods and standards.

Sample Response

Situation:
While travelling in India, I learnt the art of Indian head massage.

Action:
When I returned to work, I began using my new skill on clients while carrying out the shampoo.

Result:
My massages were becoming such a success, that my manager approached me to request that I train my colleagues. Naturally, I was honoured to oblige.

Describe a new idea or suggestion that you made to your supervisor

Sample Response

Situation:
When I was working at Trina's Hair Salon, I had noticed that a lot of our clients wore nail extensions.

Action:
Convinced that the service would be an improvement to our already successful salon, I carried out extensive independent research before presenting the idea to my manager.

Result:
After carrying out her own research, she liked the idea so much that she decided to go ahead with the new service. Within a couple of months, the service was up and running, and we experienced a dramatic increase in new clientele and revenue. I even got a small bonus in my pay packet for my involvement.

27 Tell me about a problem you encountered and the steps you took to overcome it

Sample Response

Situation:
Early in my freelancing career, I experienced several clients who turned up late to their appointments. Some even forgot about their appointments altogether. Rather than just simply being an inconvenience, it was wasting my time and money.

Action:
I considered my options and decided that the best solution would be to send out reminder cards a few days prior to client appointments. For the repeat offenders, I would enforce a late cancellation fee.

Result:
This decision drastically cut the number of late arrivers, and I have never since had a no-show.

28 Tell me about a problem that didn't work out

Evaluation

No matter how hard we try, there are some instances where a problem just doesn't work out. To say otherwise will not sound honest or credible.

In answering this question, you need to first ensure that the problem was a minor one which had no negative or lasting impact on the company, a colleague or a customer. Try to accentuate the positives and keep your answer specific. Itemize the steps you took to deal with the problem and make it clear that you learnt from the experience.

Sample Response

Situation:
Shortly after I began freelancing, my bank returned a client's cheque to me through lack of funds.

Action:
At first, I was sure it was a mistake caused through an oversight on the part of my client. I made a number of calls, left several messages and even attempted a visit to the clients home, all to no avail.

Several weeks passed and it was clear that I was chasing a lost cause. At this point, I had to decide whether to write off the debt and blacklist the client or visit the Citizens' Advice for advice on retrieving the funds.

Result:
After careful consideration of all the factors involved, I decided to write the debt off as a learning experience.

Reflection:
In hindsight, I realise it was a silly mistake that could easily have been avoided. I have never repeated this error since as I now wait for the funds to clear before carrying out a service.

29 Have you ever taken the initiative to solve a problem that was above your responsibilities?

Evaluation

Those candidates who demonstrate that they use their initiative and put in extra effort to provide a better and more complete service will surely be looked upon favourably.

Sample Response

Situation:
It had been quite an uneventful afternoon when, all of the sudden, in walked an obviously frantic customer.

From what I could understand, her laptop had contracted a virus while connected to the internet and the system now failed to respond to any commands.

Being a self-employed web designer, the customer was naturally very concerned about the potential loss of data, and earnings.

Unfortunately, while the laptop was still within warranty, it was beyond the companies scope and had to be sent to the manufacturer for restoration. My colleagues, while polite, but could only offer assistance as far as sending the laptop to the manufacturer.

Action:
I could sense the customer was becoming increasingly distressed and, having had previous training in system restoration, I was confident that I could at least safely extract the data from the hard drive.

After talking the customer through the procedure, she granted her permission and I proceeded.

Result:
After some 45 minutes of fiddling with wires and hard drives, the customer's data had been successfully, and safely, extracted. The customer gasped a big sigh of relief as we packaged the laptop off to the manufacturer for repair.

Several weeks later, my line manager received a letter from the customer complimenting my efforts.

Reflection:
I was really pleased that a little effort made such a big difference.

30 When have you made a bad decision?

Evaluation

We all make decisions that we regret, and to say otherwise will not sound honest or credible.

The recruiter will be assessing whether you have the character to admit and take responsibility for your mistake, whether your decision had a negative impact on customers or the company, and whether you learnt from this mistake?

In answering this question, you need to first ensure that the mistake was a minor one, which had no negative or lasting impact on the company, a colleague or a customer. Try to accentuate the positives and keep your answer specific. Itemize what you did and how you did it. Finally, you need to make it clear that you leant from the mistake and will be certain not to repeat it.

Situation:

Early in my freelance career, I was approached by a salesman who was promoting a protein conditioning system. He described the system as "The newest technology to emerge from years of research. Guaranteed to help heal, strengthen, and protect".

Although I was excited by the concept, I did have my concerns that the system sounded too good to be true. However, the salesman had all the official paperwork to back up his claims, and the literature was thorough and well presented. All these things, combined with the company's full money-back guarantee, made it appear to be a win-win situation, and a risk worth taking. So I invested.

Following my investment, I decided to test the system out on training heads before taking the system public. Unfortunately, several months of using the system passed with no obvious benefits.

Action:

Disappointed with the product, I decided to pursue the full money back guarantee, but the sales number was not recognised, and my letters were returned unopened. Even their website had mysteriously vanished. I soon came to the realisation that I had been taken in by an elaborate scam.

I contacted the Citizens Advice Bureau and Trading Standards, but there was little they could do to retrieve my funds.

Result:

Unfortunately, I never recovered my costs and had to put the mistake down to a learning experience.

Reflection:

Unfortunately, it really was my fault. I should have trusted my gut instinct and carried out thorough research before making my decision. It is a mistake I shall never repeat.

What was the biggest challenge you have faced?

Sample Response

Situation:
To be honest, giving up smoking was the biggest challenge. I never thought I could do it, and I had made dozens of attempts that ended in failure.

Action:
Determined not to give in to my withdrawals, I decided I needed an incentive that would pull me through the tough times. Being sponsored for a worthy cause was the perfect solution.

Result:
With a good cause in mind, the following three months were easier than on previous occasions. Not only have I come out the other end a non-smoker, I also managed to raise £2464.00 for Childline.

Reflection:
Since I gave up smoking, I have gained so much personal insight, and I deal with potentially stressful situations at work so much more effectively now, I feel more energetic, more mentally alert and far calmer now than I ever did before.

HYPOTHETICAL &
ROLE PLAY
SCENARIOS

Hypothetical

Hypothetical questions present candidates with difficult real-life situations, where almost any answer can be challenged.

A good way to approach these questions is to consider the feelings of everyone involved, and think about the implications for your colleagues and the airline.

Prove to the recruiters that you would be proactive and do your best to resolve the situation using your own initiative, whilst remembering that you could ask for the help of the more experienced crew if necessary.

If you have followed these guidelines and are still challenged, the recruiter may be testing your ability to manage conflict or stress. Bear in mind that if you are not cabin crew yet, you cannot really be expected to know the best reply so do not be tricked into entering into an argument with the recruiter.

In either case it is important to remain calm and focused, and to demonstrate that, although you appreciate there are many aspects to each situation, you would always be trying to find acceptable solutions.

If you really can't think of a solution, you can simply say, "That is a new area for me so I am afraid I can't really answer that, but I enjoy acquiring new knowledge and I do learn quickly."

You are in flight at 30,000 feet. How would you handle a passenger if he became irate about his lost baggage?

"At 30,000 feet, there is not a lot you can do about the baggage, so the problem at hand is reassuring the passenger and avoiding further disruption.

First, I would try to manoeuvre the passenger somewhere more private where they can explain the situation. I would then apologise for the mishandling, and offer to assist on the ground by escorting him to the proper people who can help."

What would you do if the seat belt signs are on due to turbulence, but a passenger gets up to go to the toilet?

"Because of the importance of passenger safety, I would advise the passenger to wait until the seat belt signs have been turned off. If the passenger really cannot wait, I will follow the corporate policy for dealing with such a situation."

How would you handle a passenger who is intoxicated?

"I would not provide any more alcoholic beverages. I would encourage food, and offer a cup of tea or coffee. If the situation worsens beyond my control, I would inform my senior and seek assistance from the other crew members."

What would you do if a commercially important passenger complained about a crying child?

"I would apologise to the passenger and offer my assistance to the guardian of the child."

How would you deal with a passenger who is scared of flying?

"Being aware of what to expect, and just realising that a plane's wings are supposed to flex and move around gently in flight, can help relieve anxiety. Similarly, the collection of bumps and bangs that always accompany a flight can be made less fearsome if they are expected. So, I would try to comfort the passenger by talking them through the flight, and reassuring them of any strange noises they may hear.

I would advise them where I can be found, and show them the call bell. I would then check on them periodically throughout the flight."

How would you deal with a passenger who is not, right but believes he is right?

"I would explain the company's rules and policies to the passenger in a calm, professional and positive manner. Hopefully, this should clarify any misconceptions that the passenger may have."

How would you handle a colleague who is being rude or racist?

"I would act immediately to put a stop to any racist or rude behaviour by making it clear to the person that their behaviour is not acceptable. If he or she continues, I would then report it to proper authority."

If you spotted a colleague doing something unethical or illegal, what would you do?

"I would act immediately to put a stop to any unethical or illegal activity. I would try to document the details of the incident and try to collect any physical evidence. Then I would report it to my senior."

What would you do if you suspect that a passenger is suspicious or a high risk to passengers?

"I would keep watch before reporting to the senior any abnormal behaviour indicating a suspicious passenger."

What would you do and how would you react in a hijacking?

"I would remain calm, and follow the emergency guidelines and procedures."

How would you act in an emergency such as a crash landing?

"As soon as I get the warning that something is going to happen, I would get a plan together in my mind. I would stay calm and in control and follow the emergency guidelines and procedures."

If you were going to Mars, what three items would you take?

"First, I would take a trained astronaut. Second, sufficient food for the journey and finally, enough fuel for the return trip."

Role-play

SCENARIOS

Role-play scenarios will bear some relation to the demands of the position, even if this is not immediately apparent. The scenarios are used to reveal key competencies required for the position and are likely to include:

Intoxicated passenger	Disorderly behaviour
Terrorist threat	Disruptive child
Toilet smoker	Abusive behaviour
Fearful passenger	Passenger complaint

The assessors don't expect you to know the answer to every possible scenario they introduce. They simply want to see how you react in challenging situations. So when taking part in any role play scenario, use the following guidelines:

- Be proactive and do your best to resolve the situation using your initiative
- Remain calm and composed
- Be direct and assertive
- Immerse yourself into the role
- Take each scenario seriously
- Devise a plan and follow it as much as possible

Here are some pointers to help you deal with some common scenarios:

Complaint

In the case of a passenger complaint, it is important that you listen to their concern without interruption. Ask questions, where appropriate, to clarify their concerns and show empathy towards their situation. If the facts warrant it, apologise for the situation, explain what action you intend to take and thank them for bringing the matter to your attention.

Fearful passenger

If a passenger is fearful of flying, be considerate of their feelings. Use a gentle and calm tone to talk them through the flight and reassure them of any sounds or sensations they may experience. Let the passenger know where you can be found and show them the call bell.

Intoxicated passenger

Offer the passenger a cup of tea or coffee and don't provide any more alcoholic drinks. You could also encourage the passenger to eat some food. Remain calm towards the passenger, but be direct and assertive in your approach. If you feel it appropriate, inform your senior and seek assistance from other crewmembers.

Sell me this pen

The interviewer may ask a question such as this in an attempt to throw you off guard and see how you react to on the spot questions. The question isn't about the product you are being asked to sell, and selling isn't a part of the job. Read between the lines and you will discover that the interviewer will be assessing: How well do you respond to pressure? How quickly can you think on your feet? Do you think before you speak? How well do you research and present information? Do you focus on the positives or negatives?

Before delving in and answering this question, demonstrate your attention to detail by asking for a few moments while you examine the product. During this period, take the opportunity to write with it. Click the pen on and off. Examine the feel of the pen as it touches the paper and look at the flow of ink. Notice everything you can that could be viewed as a benefit. Is the ink vivid? Does it glide smoothly across the paper? Does it feel substantial in your hand? Is is light and easy to hold? Is it disposable and inexpensive to replace?

Once you have a good understanding of the pen, reiterate these positive benefits back to the interviewer.

If the interviewer throws an objection, they are looking to see how you handle adversity. In this instance, remain calm, acknowledge the objection, and restate the benefits as appropriate. Remember, the task is unimportant, but the way you react is vital.

MAKE A
SUCCESSFUL
CLOSE

Have you stretched the truth today to gain a favourable outcome?

"Absolutely not. I haven't tried to be someone I am not, because I wouldn't want to get the job that way. To do so would be such a short term gain because eventually I would be found out."

How would you respond if we told you that you have been unsuccessful on this occasion?

"Naturally, I will be a disappointed if I do not secure this job with you because it is something I really want, I feel ready for it, and I have had plenty to contribute. However, I am not one to give up quickly. I will think about where I went wrong and how I could have done better, and I would then take steps towards strengthening my candidacy."

What would you say if I said your skills and experience were below the requirements of this job?

"I would ask what particular aspects of my skills and experience you felt were lacking and address each one of those areas with examples of where my skills and experiences do match your requirements. I would expect that after this discussion you would be left in no doubt about my ability to do this job."

Aren't you overqualified for this position?

"I wouldn't say that I am overqualified, but certainly fully qualified. With more than the minimal experience, I offer immediate returns on your investment. Don't you want a winner with the skill sets and attitudes to do just that?"

What question could I ask that would intimidate you?

"I can't think of any question that would intimidate me. This is probably the most intimidating question."

How would you rate me as a recruiter?

"First, I'd give you high marks for your people skills. You helped me feel at ease right away, which made it easier for me to answer the questions. I'd also rate you highly on the creativity of the questions, and their thoroughness. By probing me as carefully as you have, you've given me a better opportunity to secure this position. You've given me a complete picture of what to expect at Emirates, and it confirms my belief that this is where I want to work."

I'm not sure you are suitable for the position. Convince me.

"I am absolutely suitable. In fact, I am confident that I am perfect for this position.

You are looking for someone who is customer focused. Well, as you can see from my résumé, I have worked in client facing roles for eight years so have had plenty of experience dealing with the various aspects. I also run a successful business that relies on customer satisfaction. The fact that I am still in business, and have a solid and increasing client base, is a clear testament to my abilities.

Furthermore, you need someone who has a calm approach, and retains their composure in the face of adversity. Again, I have demonstrated this capability on several occasions throughout my career.

Beyond this, I have a friendly and optimistic character. I am hard working, I thrive on challenges and will always strive to deliver the highest standard of service to your passengers.

I am confident that my skills, experience and personal qualities will complement your existing team and allow me to make a positive contribution to the airline's ongoing success."

So you do still wish us to consider you for this position?

"Absolutely! Having had this chance to meet you and learn more about the airline and position, I am even more eager than before. I am convinced that this is the opportunity I am seeking, and I know I can make a positive contribution."

Would you take this job if we offered it to you?

"Yes, definitely. I was eager as soon as I saw the job opening on your web site. More than that though, actually meeting potential colleagues and finding out more about the airline and the position has clarified still further what an exciting challenge it would be to work here."

When are you available to start if offered the position?

"I have the energy and enthusiasm to start straight away. All I need is a week's notice and I'm ready."

Do you have any reservations about working here?

"I don't have any reservations at this point. I see this position as a fine opportunity, and the airline as one I would be proud to be an employee of."

Can we contact previous employers for references?

"Yes, absolutely. I'm confident that all my references will be favourable and will confirm what we've discussed here today."

Ask the
RIGHT QUESTIONS

This section of the interview is a real chance for you to shine and set yourself apart from all the other candidates. Therefore, it is a good idea to prepare one or two intelligent questions in advance.

The questions you ask, and how you ask them, say a lot about you, your motives, your depth of knowledge about the airline and the position itself.

Guidelines

The questions you ask should follow these guidelines:

- » Don't ask questions that could be easily answered through your own research.
- » Ask questions which demonstrate a genuine interest in and knowledge of the airline and the position.
- » Demonstrate that you know just that little bit more than is required.

Question About Suitability

Asking recruiters to raise their concerns about your suitability will provide you with an opportunity to follow up and reassure the recruiter.

» Do you have any reservations about my ability to do this job?

» What do you foresee as possible obstacles or problems I might have?

» Is there anything else I need to do to maximise my chances of getting this job?

» How does my background compare with others you have interviewed?

» Is there anything else you'd like to know?

» What do you think are my strongest assets and possible weaknesses?

» Do you have any concerns that I need to clear up in order to be a considered candidate?

Questions About the Recruiter

Asking recruiters about their views and experience in the job or working with the airline will demonstrate your genuine interest and motives.

» How did you find the transition in relocating to a Muslim country? (This question shows that you have researched Dubai and are interested in more than sunbathing and having a holiday)

» Why did you choose to work at Emirates?

» What is it about Emirates that keeps you working here?

» It sounds as if you really enjoy working here, what have you enjoyed most about working for Emirates?

General Questions

» How would you describe the company culture?

» I feel my background and experience are a good fit for this position, and I am very interested. What is the next step?

No Questions

» I did have plenty of questions, but we've covered them all during our discussions. I was particularly interested in ... but we've dealt with that thoroughly.

» I had many questions, but you've answered them all you have been so helpful. I'm even more excited about this opportunity than when I applied.

Questions to Avoid

You should avoid asking questions such as those following as they will make you appear selfishly motivated.

» How many day's holiday allowances will I receive?

» What is the salary?

» When will I receive a pay increase?

» How many free flights will my family receive?

» Can I request flights to ...?

Also be sure to avoid questions related to controversial subjects, such as terrorism, religion and political unrest.

THE
CONCLUSION
WHAT NEXT?

What happens

NEXT?

Following the final interview, Emirates aim to follow up with candidates within two to eight weeks. This is the hardest part of the whole process, and it is unlikely that you will sleep soundly as you wait of the results of your interview.

If you are successful, you can expect to receive a job offer from the recruitment department by email and a telephone call, dubbed the 'Golden Call', within the noted time frame.

There are various pre-joining clearances at this stage that need to be completed. These mandatory checks include:

- A pre-employment medical test – to be conducted in your home country at your own expense
- Reference checks
- Joining forms - you will be advised by your assigned recruitment contact on how to access these forms.

Once the mandatory checks and supplementary steps of the process have been completed, the Human Resources Service Centre (HRSC) will make the necessary arrangements to deliver the employment contract and relevant documentation. You will also be given final clearance to resign from your current employer and subsequently, a copy of your accepted resignation may be requested.

In some cases employment contracts will be dispatched to you prior to the clearances being given, however, the contract terms clearly state that the validity of the employment contract is subject to obtaining these pre-joining clearances. If you receive the contract prior to clearance being given, do not resign from your current employment until you are formally advised the recruitment team.

Coping with

SETBACKS

It may seem counter intuitive to provide coping strategies for rejection in an interview guidance book, however, in an industry such as this, where supply exceeds demand, rejection is an unfortunate outcome that some candidates will ultimately face.

So, rather than be crushed by this outcome, I have put together the following tips for coping with, learning from and moving forward following a setback.

Prepare

The popular saying 'Prepare for the worst, but hope for the best' certainly applies in interview scenarios. If you attend the interview with an open mind, your attitude will be more relaxed, you will be better prepared and your coping abilities will be greatly enhanced.

Assess

Faced with rejection, it can be easy to misplace blame on yourself, others or on the general circumstances. But, if you are to learn and grow from your experience, you must be objective and logical in your assessment, rather than making rash and unsubstantiated assumptions.

Firstly, you need to reflect on your own performance to establish any possible areas for improvement. You can then make adjustments as necessary and shift your focus to the next opportunity.

Firstly, you need to reflect on your own performance to establish any possible areas for improvement. In this assessment, you could ask:

- Did I dress appropriately?
- How did I sound?
- Did I arrive on time?
- Did I remember to smile?
- Did I appear confident and relaxed?
- Could my answers have been improved?
- Did I maintain appropriate eye contact?
- Did I establish rapport with the recruiter?

If this assessment identifies any weaknesses, you can make adjustments as necessary and shift your focus to the next opportunity.

Accept

Sometimes factors exist that are beyond your control and the unfortunate outcome may not have been directly influenced by your performance at all. In this instance, all you can do is accept the outcome and shift your focus to the next opportunity.

Be positive

Whatever the reason for rejection, it is important to treat each setback as a learning experience. So, don't become obsessive or overly critical, keep an open mind and be open to change if necessary. By handling the setback in this way, you will move forward and succeed much more quickly.

I would love
TO HEAR FROM YOU

If you have enjoyed reading this guide and have found it useful, I would love to hear from you, so please consider leaving your feedback.

www.CabinCrew.Guide

Where dreams are made

Facebook

Bibliography

RECOMMENDED READING

English for Cabin Crew
By Terence Gerighty and Shon Davis
ISBN: 0462098737

Express Series English for Cabin Crew: A short, specialist English course.
(Oxford Business English)
By Lewis Lansford and Sue Ellis
ISBN: 0194579573

Also be sure to check out the specialist TOEFL books, as these will provide advanced guidance.

Printed in Great Britain
by Amazon.co.uk, Ltd.,
Marston Gate.